OUR JIMMY

A CELEBRATION OF JAMES YOUNG

ANDREW McKINNEY was born in Belfast in 1961.
Educated at the Royal Belfast Academical Institution, he has worked for Short Brothers and Harland & Wolff. He is currently employed as a computer engineer and professional web designer.

While studying for a Higher National Diploma in information technology, he designed the popular James Young tribute website, ourjimmy.com

Andrew is married with two children and lives in Belfast. This is his first book.

OUR JIMMY

A Celebration of James Young

Andrew McKinney

Foreword by Brian Kennedy

THE BREHON PRESS
BELFAST

First published 2003 by The Brehon Press Ltd,

111 Brooke Drive, Belfast BT11 9NJ,

County Antrim, Northern Ireland

ISBN: 0 9544867 0 6

Front and back cover (middle and bottom) photography: Stanley Matchett MBE
Back cover photograph (top): Leslie Stuart
Cover design: Ron Kelly
Designed by December Publications
Printed in Ireland by Betaprint, Dublin

ACKNOWLEDGEMENTS

It's true to say that this book would not have been possible without the help of a lot of people. First and foremost, I would like to thank my wife, Deborah, and sons, Corey and Robbie, for their continual support for this project, which they know is very close to my heart.

The following people have my sincere thanks for giving me their time and consideration:

Firstly, the lovely Jean Brown (neé Lundy), a wonderful lady with wonderful stories: how can you have a proper James Young book without Emily Beattie?

Of Jimmy's close circle of friends, I would like to thank Leonard McNeill, Frank Crummey, Ivan Martin, Olivia Nash, and Philip Mulholland. Philip didn't allow the fact that he lives on the other side of the world to hinder his efforts to assist me. I hope that this finished publication embodies the trust and patience you all showed me.

My eternal gratitude is extended to the multi-talented Brian Kennedy ("the singer fella with the high voice") who has displayed a real generosity of spirit in his splendid foreword.

I am indebted to George Doherty, of Emerald Music, for permission to reproduce extracts from Jimmy's recorded material and Stanley Matchett, who certainly came up trumps with his excellent photographs.

I would also like to voice my appreciation to the following individuals and companies who all contributed towards making the book a reality: BBC Northern Ireland, John Bennett, George Jones, Peter Lloyd, Grainne Loughran and Lynda Atcheson at the BBC NI Archive in Cultra, Keith Beattie at the Ballymoney Borough Museum, Tom Norton and George Curry at BIFHE, Kathleen Bell at the *Irish News*, Walter McAuley and Niall Sherry at the *Belfast Telegraph*, the Belfast Central Library Newspaper Archive, Ophelia Byrne at the Linen Hall Library, Yvonne Friers, Charles Oakley, Suzanne Lyle at the Arts Council of Northern Ireland, William Caulfield, Tony Brown, Trevor Badger, Belfast City Council, Bre Dearnaley, John Clancy, the *Belfast News Letter*, Dessie McKeown, Jimmy Johnston, Maurice Beckett, Frank Kennedy of the *Irish Showbands Archive*, Joyce Burrell, Pat Catney at the Kitchen Bar, Lorraine Fannin, Suzy Lundy, Rob Batsford, John Trew, Patrick Scully, John Keyes, Patrick Ramsey, Dennis Reynolds, Richard Mills, Ian McCartney, Robert Thompson, Stephen Davidson, Edith Gibson, Hugh Sterrett and Jim Sherrard at Castlereagh Borough Council.

Finally, I would like to express thanks to my publishers, Brendan Anderson and Damian Keenan at The Brehon Press, for their tireless efforts in pulling all of the pieces together to create a marvellous tribute to a unique individual.

PICTURE CREDITS

Photographs and illustrations have been reproduced by kind permission of the following: Stanley Matchett Photography, Belfast (pp10, 72, 73, 75, 76, 79, 80, 87, 88, 92, 94, 95, 98, 99, 101, 115, 116, 117, 133); Belfast Telegraph (pp39, 68, 82, 85, 86, 90, 108, 109, 111, 114, 116, 124); Keith Beattie, Ballymoney Borough Museum (pp12, 129); Charles Oakley and the Arts Council of Northern Ireland Collection (p136); BBC Northern Ireland Archive (pp37, 38, 59); Yvonne Friers (pp77, 100, 106, 107); Philip Mulholland (pp62, 63, 69, 78); Pat Catney (p20); Leonard McNeill (pp53, 57, 70); Leslie Stuart (pp42, 43); Peter Lloyd (p87); Dessie McKeown (p125); Flo Hunter (p12); May Thompson (p59); David Hull Promotions (pp130, 131); Andrew McKinney (pp92, 93, 129, 130); and Frank Kennedy (p104).

A NOTE ON SOURCES

The author and publishers wish to extend their gratitude to the following people who gave up their time to relate their stories and memories of Jimmy, without which this book would not have seen the light of day: Jean Brown, Philip Mulholland, Leonard McNeill, Maurice Beckett, Jimmy Johnston, Dessie McKeown, Peter Lloyd, Ivan Martin, Olivia Nash, William Caulfield, Stanley Matchett, George Doherty, Joyce Burrell, and John Keyes.

Many additional quotes from Jimmy himself are reproduced here from two excellent interviews written in the 1960s: the first, by John Trew for *Cityweek*; the second, by Rob Batsford for the *Sunday News*. Unfortunately, these newspapers are now defunct, but it is hoped that both journalists receive and accept our thanks.

BBC Northern Ireland's invaluable programme, 'Our Jimmie', in the *Home Truths* series, provided additional information.

Of the books used, Jack Hudson's *The Entire Company* (Blackstaff Press, 1975), was indispensable, as was John Keyes' *Going Dark: Two Ulster Theatres* (Lagan Press, 2001). Background material on the Troubles was drawn from the essential *Lost Lives: The stories of the men, women and children who died as a result of the Northern Ireland Troubles* (Mainstream Publishing, 1999) by David McKittrick, Seamus Kelters, Brian Feeney, and Chris Thornton.

Contextual material and information was sourced from back issues of the *Belfast Telegraph*, the *Irish News*, *Cityweek*, the *Sunday News*, and the *Belfast News Letter*.

Extracts from monologues, sketches and songs are reproduced by kind permission of George Doherty at Emerald Music. The monologue in Chapter 10 is reproduced by kind permission of William Caulfield.

The authors and publishers have made every reasonable effort to contact the copyright holders of photographs and other material reproduced in the book. If any involuntary infringement of copyright has occurred, sincere apologies are offered and the owners of such copyright are requested to contact the publishers.

Dedicated to Deb, Core and Rob

FOREWORD

Here we are in 2003.

Belfast is unrecognisable in this new millennium of confidence, extra virgin olive oil, croissants and tall skimmed lattes, compared to the late 60s, 70s and early 80s, when the only place you could get a cup of tea and a biscuit was in your granny's.

They say you can tell a lot about a country if you look at its famous people. Reading about James Young's life gives renewed meaning to the spirit of survival in the most difficult of times, and it's a testament to his powerful instincts that his work is as moving and relevant now as it ever was. Who else had the comedic balls to parade all of our bigoted insecurities and fears under the biggest magnifying glass he could find – the TV and the stage? And he did it right under our very noses, educating us in the process, and reducing the hardest of hearts to tears of laughter.

I remember meeting Quentin Crisp in New York in the mid-90s, and it dawned on me that he was the kind of character Jimmy might have invented if he'd still been with us. Young's appetite for expressing humanity in all of its guises was insatiable.

I wish I was privileged enough to say I'd seen Jimmy live, but I can't. So how do we attempt to keep his memory appropriately lit? With the help of Andrew McKinney's wonderful book, we are breathing new life into this extraordinary individual. After reading it, I felt closer to knowing the man who is still unequalled in his originality and versatile brilliance. For me, it's impossible not to imagine his impish grin in the clouds above Belfast's City Hall as he regards how far we've come and how much further we still have to go.

Jimmy was undoubtedly ahead of his time but right on the money all at once, like real geniuses always are. This book is a fitting tribute to a Quare Fella. I know they say only the good die young, but he left us too soon.

Read on!

BRIAN KENNEDY
12 August 2003

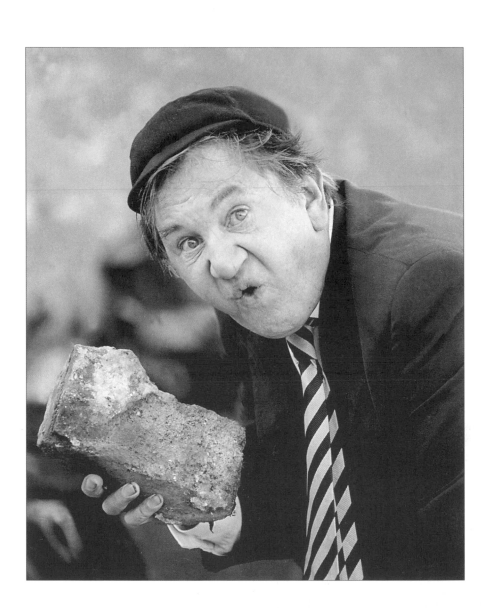

1

At a secret location in Northern Ireland, known only to a select few, there stand two mature cherry trees.

In the space between these trees can be found a small plaque with an inscription which reads simply: 'To Suzy's godfathers'.

The Suzy mentioned was the first grandchild of a fine comic actress by the name of Jean Lundy. The godfathers were two of Jean's closest friends, and the plaque was her own private way of leaving a lasting memorial in their honour.

One of these friends was an Englishman called Jack Hudson. The other was a comic actor who, at the time of his death, had become such an integral part of Ulster people's lives that he was fondly referred to as 'Our Jimmy'.

His name was James Young and this is his story.

Alexander Young, Jimmy's father

James Alexander Young was born at 33 Union Street, a nondescript terrace house in Ballymoney, on 23 June 1918.

It is one of the few facts about Jimmy's early years which can be stated with any degree of confidence. Much is shrouded in mystery and many basic facts have been lost beyond hope of recovery. An entertainer and not a writer, Jimmy was never to publish his autobiography and a lot of his newspaper interviews were essentially puff pieces to promote new stage, radio and television shows. Anecdotes about his early years were precisely that. Their point was to amuse, not necessarily inform.

James Alexander was to be the last addition to the family and, perhaps importantly for the budding comedian, the only boy. While never

Ballymoney, circa. 1918

33 Union Street, Ballymoney as it looks today

less than fond of his father, Alexander, the lasting and dominating influence in his early life was his mother, Grace. With three older sisters – Ann, Margaret and May – and a dominant mother, it could be surmised that the womenfolk held the upper hand in the household. Indeed, like many an Ulster home, while it was nominally the husband or the father who was head of the household, it was the women who held the family together.

Young's father was, at the time of Jimmy's birth, a bread server, delivering for a small baker's shop to the residents of the County Antrim market town. It was a place which was to be forever close to Jimmy's heart – and his comedy. Although he only lived in the town for the first few months of his infancy, family ties and memories meant that the Belfast man *par excellence* always considered Ballymoney his home. The rural Ulster-Scots burr and, of course, the legendary canniness of Ulster country folk with regard to keeping their hard earned pounds, shillings and pence, were to become a mainstay of his comic repertoire. In such popular characters as the Ballymena Cowboy and Emily Beattie's Auntie, we see affectionate recreations of the people he and his kin knew intimately. As in all his characters, the humour was generous with no place for mean-spiritedness or malice.

Jimmy outside Fernwood Street, Belfast with his pet dog, Jess

Jimmy's birth was against a background of gaslit streets and hiring fairs. Ballymoney was still in the process of electrification and, despite the presence of Balnamore Mill, one of the largest linen mills outside of Belfast, the town's existence still revolved very much around the local farming community. In 1918, Ballymoney writer George Shiels was working on his first play, *Moodie in Manitoba*, above his travel agent's shop in the town, and the whole community was reeling from the loss of many of its young men in the First World War, which was just drawing to a close.

The arrival of a fourth mouth to feed must have been a hard financial blow to a family living on a simple bread server's wage. Times were difficult and making a living precarious. Britain was exhausted financially, militarily and emotionally. Thousands of men were pouring back into the country from the army, desperate to find work and normality. Lucrative government war work was winding down. In southern Ireland, republicans fought an increasingly bitter guerrilla war against the British. In the north, Ulster was preparing to fight Home Rule, and sectarian tensions were rising. A new, less certain, world was in the process of being born.

It is probable that the Youngs were forced to leave Ballymoney in search of a more secure future. Belfast, still basking in the glorious afterglow of being one of the great industrial cities of the British Empire, drew families like a magnet in search of work and a better, more civilised way of life. The greatest shipyard in the world, major rope and brick works, mills and factories too numerous to mention – the lure proved irresistible to Alexander Young and his family.

Probably because of his previous employment, Jimmy's father quickly found a job as stableman at Inglis & Co Bakery in the Markets area. It was just one of the many great Belfast bakeries whose names are intertwined with the history of the city: Hughes', Kennedy's, and Ormo, to name but three of the better known. The bakeries poured out bread, baps, Paris buns and cheap pastries to feed the teeming population of Belfast. In the days before supermarkets and vans, the bread had to be distributed to hundreds of small corner shops and direct to the small terrace houses of the factory workers. All the major bakeries had considerable stables.

The family's home was 26 Fernwood Street, close to the Ormo premises, and little more than a stale bap's throw from the main Inglis bakery in Eliza Street. Later, they were to move to Ava Park, also within the shadow of the bakery.

The Youngs were not completely alone in the big city. Jimmy's maternal grandmother was born and still lived in Donegall Pass. As was the ingrained Belfast habit, familial generations lived within short walking

Jimmy, aged five

Jimmy and his mother, Grace, on holiday in Bangor

distance, popping in and out of each other's houses with the latest news and gossip. It was, of course, a network of support strengthened by Belfast's famed sense of community. In a world of just a few streets, everyone knew everyone and life had its own distinct rituals and rhythms. Sickness and health, wealth and destitution, trials and tribulation – everybody knew everybody else's business.

It was, in many ways, an ideal childhood for a would-be comedian whose stock in trade would be to observe people. As he was to recall in interview after interview, Jimmy was endlessly fascinated by people, watching them, drawing comic inspiration from those around him. Yet, he was always denying that characters were drawn directly from individuals. His characters, he would stoutly maintain, were composites – a gesture borrowed from this person, a turn of phrase from that, a little telling foible from another. More than just mimicking, he absorbed the life going on around him.

Whenever his family's friends dropped in on No 26, Jimmy would perch himself in the living room, just watching and, in his child's mind, already working out basic scripts for the skits he would improvise as soon as the front door closed, leaving him to an appreciative audience of one: his mother. She and the thousands of local women just like her were to be his best, his most appreciative, his most understanding audience. In later years, he often recalled with a certain pride that his mother was often bent double laughing at his mimicry, his sharp tongue and his sense of the absurd underlying the everyday.

'Every time we had visitors,' Jimmy told journalist John Trew, 'my mother used to go into convulsions at the gestures I made behind our guests' backs. She was a very warm and good-humoured person and she responded to all my visual jokes. In the end she had to draw me, on some pretence, into the kitchen and warn me that I would have to cut it out, as she found it difficult to take the people seriously after my mimicking their little mannerisms.'

It was, perhaps, inevitable, that his mother's approval would mean much to the young Jimmy. He was, by his own admission, not a street ragamuffin, beloved of Belfast memoirs, constantly getting into fights and scraps. He was a sensitive child, at his happiest in the world of his imagination.

'Even as a very young boy,' he said, 'I was completely

The Young Family, minus one sister

fascinated by theatrical illusion and comic acting. I was never terribly interested in going out to play in the street. Instead, I used to go upstairs and put on hats and bedspreads and parade in front of the dressing table mirror.'

Jimmy's relationship with his mother was always the most important in his life: 'People would tell me that I was tremendously like her. And it's very true because my sense of humour was just the same as hers. She was a marvellous woman and I adored her. She had white hair from a very early age, which was very attractive, and laughing grey eyes. She also had a gorgeous sense of humour and a most infectious laugh, and she always saw the funny things in people.'

Always by nature guarded about revealing the 'real' James Young beyond the laughter and the footlights, there seems no doubt that his childhood was a happy if somewhat unmelodramatic one. While drawn more to his mother, his father was also fondly remembered as a focus of quiet fun.

Responsible for looking after the Inglis stable of dray horses, Alexander Young would take a real, if slightly knowing pride, in his cares. Indeed, his identification with his horses would occasionally lead to the embarrassment of his son, self-conscious as all young adolescent children are.

'My father travelled to work … at an outrageously early hour every morning. In those days, in the late 20s, Inglis had about 300 horses for their bread vans and it was my father's job to look after their wellbeing. He had to pass the horses as fit before they went out pulling the bread and milk carts and such like. This was before they had the electric carts.

'Sometimes, walking down the road with him, I would get a bit embarrassed when he would stop a van and say, "How's Daisy? She's got a weak knee, that one." It might have been two years since he last treated her, but he would know.'

Jimmy would often joke: 'We never had a doctor come to our house. If ever we were ill, my father would prescribe half a horse pill and a rub down with horse liniment as his standard remedy for any ailment from a sore back to a common cold, or just malingering through not wanting to go to school.'

Prescriptions for horse pills aside, it was, in its way, an idyllic existence. The product of loving, down-to-earth parents who brought up their children well, but not too strictly, Young could not remember being in any serious trouble as a child.

'I wasn't one of those kids who were always breaking windows or missing out on school. We didn't live in luxury by any means, but we

Belfast's Empire Theatre, where Jimmy saw his first stage show

weren't in any degree of poverty either. My father had a steady job and life was fairly even and untroubled.'

His days at Cooke Church School, just off Belfast's Ravenhill Road, were similarly happy, contented and uneventful. The only subject he showed any real interest in – or aptitude for – was English. Often he would have read the class's current 'reader' from cover to cover, well before any of the other boys had progressed past the first chapter. It was a habit that often attracted the attention of his teacher.

Having already read the first book, he used to take the next one with him to the class so that he wouldn't get bored. He would then devour that one while the other pupils were being instructed to read aloud. The teacher would inevitably catch him on, shouting, 'Young, carry on from where the last boy finished!'

Amazingly, Jimmy was always able to do so, reciting from memory the correct passage from the book. This retentive memory was, of course, a boon during his theatrical career. Indeed, it would later become something of a party piece as he astounded friends and acquaintances by recounting great chunks of dialogue from plays that he had performed in years before.

Jimmy's was a traditional Presbyterian childhood. A member of the 8th Boys Brigade, he also attended Cooke Centenary Church on Park Road.

But it was only natural, perhaps, for such an imaginative child with a gift for mimicry that Jimmy became fascinated by the theatre and the great music hall tradition. And, it must be said, Belfast was a city that more than adequately catered for that fascination. The streets were festooned with variety theatres and entertainment venues. The Grand Opera House and the Hippodrome were the main palaces of variety, existing cheek by jowl in Great Victoria Street. But there were others: the Alhambra in North Street; the Empire Theatre off Victoria Square; the Alexandra at the corner of Grosvenor Road and Sandy Row; the Royal in Castle Lane; and a venue known simply as The Music Hall in Chichester Street, to name but a few.

All too willing to be starstruck, every time Jimmy went to a show, he could think and talk of little else for days afterwards. At home, he would continually act out the parts of the show that he remembered. It was a love affair that was to last the whole of his life. And, as in so many aspects of his life, it was a love encouraged and stimulated by his mother. She took her only son to as many shows as possible and this common interest formed an even closer bond between them. The forays out together were not special occasions for the pair but an organic part of their day-to-day routine. Weekly and twice-weekly outings – evenings, afternoon performances, Saturday matinees – where, for a couple of 'd' or sixpence, they could be entertained and given more material for gossip to share either between themselves or with their neighbours.

Jimmy's father was more interested in football but, although he brought Jimmy to quite a few matches, the sight of 22 men kicking a ball about didn't evoke the same magic for his son as live theatre did.

It seems that Alexander never expressed disappointment at his son's failure to become more involved in his world. But, as Jimmy would say again and again, both his parents were remarkable in giving him the freedom to go his own way. Although Grace Young, like Jimmy, loved the variety theatre, she never pointed her son towards a life on the boards.

'My mother had a wonderful liking for the theatre but that's not why I decided to get involved myself. She never pushed me into it. She never influenced you and said you must do this or you must do that. She taught you good manners but she never said I want you to be a doctor, I want you to be a dentist. She believed that you grew up and you eventually made your own mind up what you wanted to do. After she took me to that first pantomime the theatre became a regular thing in my life.'

Jimmy remembered clearly that first visit to the Empire Theatre at the age of six. For that day, he saw the comedian who was to be his model and talisman: Jimmy O'Dea.

O'Dea was, undoubtedly, Ireland's greatest comedian in the early part of the twentieth century. A star recognised wherever he went, he had toured Ireland and England extensively for many years, starting in the early 1920s. As well as being the main attraction at many music halls, he was also a small-scale film star. His silent films, *Wicklow Gold* and *Penny Paradise*, packed out cinemas across the land. Additionally, he was well known for his Athlone radio shows and his gramophone recordings of songs and monologues such as *Hands Across the Border*.

The memory of that Empire show was to stay with James Young all his life.

'To me, this was a fantastic experience that I have never forgotten. I remember the lighting especially and the main part of the show, I can recall, was when Jimmy O'Dea first came on to the stage on a prop camel.'

After this, Jimmy always made sure that whenever O'Dea's pantomimes came to the Opera House, or one of his comedy revues was playing at the Empire Theatre, he would always be there to watch him.

Maybe Jimmy was also a fan of O'Dea's regular stage partner, Albert Sharpe. Sharpe was not only funny – in itself a big attraction for Jimmy –

but local. Born on Belfast's Springfield Road, Sharpe's accent was unmistakable even from the cheapest of seats. He would later go on to establish himself as a considerable film star and character actor in the likes of *Brigadoon, Royal Parade* and *The Day They Robbed the Bank of England*. His film career peaked in 1959 when he starred in Disney's *Darby O'Gill and the Little People*, playing the eponymous Darby to O'Dea's King of the Leprechauns.

But it was always O'Dea that Jimmy would return to as his chief inspiration. Like the mature James Young, O'Dea was a master of comic female impersonation. In the 1920s, he created his most memorable character, Biddy Mulligan. Some of Jimmy's best-loved creations, such as Mrs O'Condriac and Orange Lil, can be traced directly back to Biddy.

O'Dea's impact on Jimmy was deep and profound and it was one the Ulster comedian always readily and openly acknowledged.

'Really, to me, (O'Dea) was not a comedian but a comedy actor. He became the character he was playing rather than just a performer speaking lines. His observations of characters was acute, from his beloved Mrs Mulligan, the "oul shawlie from the Coombe", to his wee railway porter in the station that was closing down. There was a terrible sadness about O'Dea's characters, for the division between comedy and tragedy is a very fine one indeed.'

It is interesting to note the distinction in Jimmy's mind between being a comedy actor and a comedian and his recognition that comedy and tragedy go hand in hand. His characters, it was often intimated, had their share of sorrow.

While O'Dea was the most obvious influence on Jimmy's work, it should not be forgotten that his brand of comedy was not at all unique. Many of the northern English music hall comic acts that Jimmy and his mother saw in their theatre visits shared the same characteristics as O'Dea – characteristics later to be picked up by Jimmy. These were strong regional characters (often in women's costume), battleaxes quick in the tongue and fond of malapropism, drawing in the audience in a conspiratorial gossip about their neighbours. Indeed, it is a tradition as old as comedy itself, surviving down to today in the work of such comedians as the late Les Dawson and even May McFettridge.

Although largely forgotten now, performers such as Jimmy James, Harry Lauder, Arthur Lucan (Old Mother Riley) and Frank Randle provided a basic template for Jimmy's brand of comedy. The point of such acts was not simply the idea of making 'jokes'. Rather, it was in the rapport between audience and performers. The scripts, if they existed at all, were merely safety nets, allowing the performer to go where he and the audience wanted.

Although besotted by the idea of the theatre and, more specifically, by the magic of getting complete strangers to burst into spontaneous laughter, Jimmy didn't have the faintest idea of how to pursue a career on the stage:

'At that early age, I didn't believe that you could go on the stage unless you had blue eyelids. Everybody on the stage had blue eyelids and I thought you had to be born with them.'

While literally failing to see behind the greasepaint to the reality of showbusiness life, Jimmy loved the glitz, the glamour and the fantasy world that was created onstage while he was watching the show. It was an escape from the bleak existence of normal Belfast life. As dole queues lengthened and the brief prosperity of the middle and late 20s gave way to the Great Depression, the theatre – or, for others, the cinema – became a much-needed refuge from the outside world.

'This is the wonderful thing about the theatre. Inside the space of a couple of hours, every member of the audience can experience every conceivable type of emotion, from fear and horror, through sadness and despair to a warm happiness. This, for me, is the fascination of the stage. Everybody knows that it's only a play but the real-life emotions are felt anyway.

'It's no wonder, therefore, that as a small boy I was completely taken in by theatrical illusion. So impressed was I that actors could hold people in their hands with such apparent ease that I actually believed that they were superhuman figures, unapproachable and untouchable. I was soon to be disillusioned.'

The boss: Mr James McCartney

One afternoon, when he was about 12, Jimmy was walking down Shaftesbury Square where, to his shock and delight, he recognised the girl who was Principal Boy in the pantomime going towards Great Victoria Street. In those days, he was much too shy to go rushing up to performers in the street to ask them for their autographs. Instead, he kept running ahead, pretending to look in shop windows, so that he could watch her coming towards him, and then he would run on another bit to keep in front of her.

'She was obviously heading for the theatre and went into a shop on the Grosvenor Road. I only had enough money on me for my bus fare home again, but I

Jimmy, the apprentice rent collector

Jimmy in an early incarnation of the comic rent collector

followed her into the shop to buy a bar of chocolate, just to be near her and hear her speak. To my horror, she leaned over the counter and asked the man in a voice quite unlike her tinkling stage tones, "Send us a bowl of stew over to the stage door between houses, will you, luv?"

'It seems funny now but I wanted to cry because my fantasy about the world of the theatre had been shattered.'

Jimmy's days at Cooke Church School ended, like so many Belfast boys, at the age of 14. And, like many, he left with no qualifications to his name. One day, spotting a 'Boy Wanted' ad in an estate agent's window, he applied for the job. After being interviewed by the boss, James McCartney, Jimmy got the position for the princely wage of nothing.

To justify this, McCartney told him, 'My boy, we are teaching you the job.' But luckily, after six months, he was given two shillings a week towards his bus fare.

His job was collecting rents from the roughest and toughest districts of the city: the Falls, the Shankill and the Crumlin Roads. It was an experience which left an indelible mark on him, witnessing up close, in the crowded back-to-backs, the joys and sorrows of the working class people of Belfast.

The areas may have been poor but they were full of vivid, colourful life. Many of the people Jimmy met during his rent collecting days would, in later years, provide inspiration for his radio, stage and small screen characters. The resilience and ingenuity of the Belfast working class stirred his comic imagination and their poverty stirred his heart.

'I suppose you could say that much of my interest in the ordinary working people of Belfast stemmed from those days as a collector. I began, unconsciously, to develop that childhood talent I had for mimicry and parody. There was any amount of material to draw upon, I can tell you. I met some of the most weird and wonderful characters on my rounds, and I've used bits and pieces of many of them on the stage but I couldn't tell you which phrase or which gesture came from a specific person.'

But Jimmy's new job also introduced him to the harsher, more brutal facts of Belfast life.

'A lot of the flats we collected for were slum properties, at very modest rents. Even so, there were hundreds of occasions I had to serve "notices to quit" because of non-payment. Being so young and impressionable, I was deeply affected by the tragic circumstances that poor people found themselves in when they were ejected. It was very often a distasteful

GRAND OPERA HOUSE

BELFAST

Programme

Grand Opera House programme from the late 30s

business. One incident has lived with me all my life and had a profound effect on me.

'I called one weeknight to a tiny one-roomed flat in Great Victoria Street where a very young girl lived alone. She was stirring a big pot of boiling soup as I presented myself at the door with the collection book.

'"The child's dead," she said. "Come and see him." There, on the bed, was a tiny white coffin and inside was the dead baby, looking like a little doll, her illegitimate son. The shock of that has never really left me.'

The actor Philip Mulholland, one of Jimmy's close friends during the 1960s, remembers him speaking of those difficult days.

'Many a time, I listened as he told stories of the characters and the hilarious things that he saw on his rounds, and the excuses people came up with for not paying the rent. On turning into certain streets on a Friday evening, he would see the lights being switched off in the houses because they knew he was coming. So it's not surprising that one of Jimmy's earliest and best-known characters was the rent collector.

'He and Jean Lundy used to do a sketch where Jimmy, as the rent man, would knock on Jean's door. Jean, as the not-so-stupid working class housewife, would end up conning him into giving her a loan which she would then use to pay the rent, keeping two quid for herself, leaving the rent man scratching his head.

'One of the things I noticed about Jimmy and his working class characters was that, although they were usually uneducated, he always gave them a certain street smart way which allowed them usually to get the better of their upper class peers.'

Some of this street smartness had obviously rubbed off on Jimmy. After two years of collecting rents, he was tired of just watching the theatre shows: he wanted to be part of them.

So, with this desire in mind, he volunteered for the Savoy Players, an English theatrical company based at the Opera House. The company had, somehow, got stranded in non-conscripted Ulster at the outbreak of the

The young Mr Young enjoying the Bangor sunshine

Second World War. An accomplished set of performers, they were to produce many acclaimed plays at their new theatrical home.

Naturally, for such an august company, Jimmy did not immediately get to act. Most of his work was to be done behind the curtain. It was the classic theatrical apprenticeship with Jimmy doing all the odd jobs, such as sweeping up and checking the props and even running errands for the actors. But slowly, he worked his way up the company ladder, reaching the exalted positions of call boy and prompt.

Jimmy recollected that not all actors had the memory skills he possessed.

'It was ironic that my first job in the professional theatre was to correct the faults of the people I had once considered infallible. I was 18 and was prompter in the Opera House for the Savoy Players.

'In the middle of one production, a veteran rep actor dried up completely and, instead of waiting for my prompt, he strode over to me and said, "What is the *line*? Dear God, what is the *play*?"

'That man was Norman Chidgey. He was the earliest influence in my career and it was he who told me to go into repertory to gain experience.'

Following the war, Chidgey returned to England to become Richard Fulton in the radio phenomenon, *Mrs Dale's Diary*. It was a role that was to make him a household name throughout Britain.

At a time when 'drama' was dominated by athletic young men with clipped English accents, Jimmy was told that his Belfast brogue would have to go. While it may be hard to imagine James Young as the lead in *Brief Encounter*, he took the advice seriously enough to attend elocution lessons. With trepidation, he clutched his sixpence in his hand on his 'way to getting elocuted', as he later described it. After an hour of dealing with a local Professor Henry Higgins, Jimmy made the fateful decision that he liked his accent just the way it was. In later years, he would always advise young actors: 'Never lose your own dialect. The words you speak are tools of your trade.'

Determined to get in front of the curtain, Jimmy joined the Youth Hostel Association Drama Group (YHADG) in 1943. As was his way, in his first year as a member, he virtually took control of the YHADG. One of the plays they performed was called *A Story for Today*, written by the Belfast playwright, Jack Loudan. It had been the first production of the recently formed Ulster Group Theatre and had proved very popular with local audiences. Following the devastation of the Belfast Blitz, the play's plot concerning evacuees touched a deep chord.

Jimmy cast the play himself, played the lead role, organised the costumes and begged, borrowed and stole the furniture and stage properties.

The YHADG had been set up by Belfast girl, Maud Magee. Her sister, Joyce Burrell, remembers Jimmy's visits to the family home.

'At the time, we lived on the Lisburn Road and James and my sister would do the rehearsals at our house. James, in those days, was very, very polite and well spoken, not the broad Belfast comedian he became in later years. So when my sister used to get out her copy of the play and my father saw her bringing it out, he would say, "Is that eedjit coming here tonight again?" Then he'd say to my mother, "Come on, we're going out."

'You see, James would engage my father in great long serious discussions because he was a very earnest young man in those days.'

Jimmy was very pleased with the production of *A Story for Today* and decided to enter it for the Ulster Drama Festival. The Festival, which was held at the Group Theatre, always attracted amateur dramatic societies from all over Northern Ireland.

The adjudicator for this particular year was the well-known Ulster playwright and biographer, St John Ervine, but Jimmy was unable to get along to the final evening to hear the results because he was prompting at the Opera House.

'My family had gone along and when I came home that night they said, "We've got news for you. You have won the individual award as the best actor of the season and St John Ervine described you as a natural comedian."'

RIGHT AGAIN BARNUM

A COMEDY by JOSEPH TOMELTY

CHARACTERS
IN ORDER OF APPEARANCE

Mrs. Marley

"Gugs" Marley   Min Milligan

Willie John Marley   Elizabeth Begley

Jack Hart   James Young

"Rabby" Marley   John F. Tyrone

Barney Brudge   John McDade

Albert Bonin   Jack O'Malley

                        Patrick Canavan

The Play produced by J. R. Mageean
(By permission of the British Broadcasting Corporation)

Settings by Dan Fitzpatrick

The action of the play takes place in the kit[chen] of a cottage outside Drogheda. Time: [

ACT I   Morning

ACT II   Afternoon

ACT III   Evening

Stage Manager   .   .

Electrician   .   .   .   Dan Fitzpatrick

Jimmy's big break in Tomelty's Right Again, Barnum

The success of *A Story for Today* fuelled Jimmy's belief that the stage was where his future lay and, to this end, he decided to organise a professional production of the show. The original cast decided to join in and he booked a suburban cinema for two nights as the venue. Again, he undertook the whole project himself and organised the sets, tickets, programmes, publicity and so on. A week before the show was to open, he was horrified to discover that he had incurred over £50 in expenses. This was equivalent to almost a year's salary from his job as a clerk, so he understandably was a bit concerned. He started a one-man sales drive and went door to door until at least all his outgoings were met. In the end, he need not have worried as the play went on to make a profit of £75.

Jimmy's production of *A Story for Today* brought him to the attention of the Ulster Group Theatre. Aware of his comedic talents and St John Ervine's justified praise for his performance, it seemed natural to offer him the part of Willie John in their presentation of Joseph Tomelty's watershed comedy, *Right Again, Barnum*.

The Group's overall importance in the history of Irish theatre cannot be stressed enough. As well as offering James Young his first steps in the professional theatre, it nurtured such major actors as R H McCandless, J G Devlin, Stephen Boyd, James Ellis, Margaret D'Arcy, Harold Goldblatt and Colin Blakely. Of equal importance were the new ideas of acting, staging and lighting which the Group brought to Ireland for the first time.

It had been formed from three different theatrical companies: the Carrickfergus Players, the North Irish Players and the Jewish Institute Players. The three had combined under the name of the Ulster Group but the original intention was to keep the companies separate, each taking the theatre in turn for their own productions.

When they first took over the Minor Hall, a small theatre located over the foyer of the Ulster Hall in Bedford Street, the Estates Committee of Belfast Corporation, who owned the lease, made them pay three months rent in advance. So a 12-week experimental run was initiated to see how things would work out.

Following a massively popular production of St John Ervine's classic, *Boyd's Shop*, it was decided that the three companies would take on a single identity and, after a consolidation period, the venue reopened as the Ulster Group Theatre in September 1941.

The driving forces behind the Group were Goldblatt, a tough businessman who was determined to look after the pennies; R H McCandless, one of Ulster's greatest comedy actors; J R Mageean and the playwright, actor and novelist, Joseph Tomelty.

Although showcasing both comedies and 'straight' plays from all over the world, the Group soon became known as the home of Ulster comedy.

Group Theatre programme from 1943

And, to be frank, the local audiences lapped up homegrown productions. After all, it was the first time that Ulster voices speaking to Ulster people had been heard on the stage.

In *Right Again, Barnum*, Jimmy's portrayal of Willie John, a role suited to his comic talents, was widely praised as a *tour de force*. A leader-off in a dance hall, Willie John is pure James Young. His talk is filled with Aspros, his sister's corn beef's legs, and his desire to become a world famous lyricist. He is, as his father, Rabby Marley says, 'like a *wemin*', if you know what I mean'. Willie John is not a world away from Derek the Window Cleaner in *The McCooeys*, a character also created by Tomelty. It was a show-stopping turn.

However, it was not all plain sailing. Frank Crummey, a close friend who also starred in many of the Group's comedies in the 1960s, recalls some first night woes.

'According to Jimmy, Harold Goldblatt was not a nice man to work for. There (Jimmy) was, a young actor busting to get on the stage but quivering with nerves at the same time. He was waiting for his big opportunity on his first night in the Group Theatre when Goldblatt came over and said, "If I could have had Allan McClelland (a well-known actor and writer of the time), you would not be playing this part tonight." This was just before he walked on the stage.'

Somehow, Jimmy put this 'vote of confidence' to the back of his mind and went onstage that night to rapturous applause, proving to Harold Goldblatt that the right person had been chosen for the role. Jimmy later recalled:

'I still had my job as a rent collector during the day and, at night, I would be

Jimmy, aged twenty

acting at the Group. It was tiring but I was so thrilled to be on the stage at last that I didn't care. *Right Again, Barnum* ran for 16 weeks and I got paid ten bob a week but you didn't get any money until the play had completed its run. That was the way the Group worked in those days.'

After the run of *Barnum* had finished, Jimmy started working at the Grand Opera House, which had its own permanent repertory company under the control of an English director called Freddie Tripp. The Second World War was still in progress and touring companies could no longer travel across the Irish Sea to Northern Ireland.

After a few weeks at the Opera House, Jimmy was offered a place in a Northern Ireland touring company headed by Ian Priestly Mitchell and his leading lady, Esme Biddell, a great Shakespearean actress of the day.

'I thought it was fabulous to be offered this but I knew it was a terrific gamble because I had no illusions about the profession. I went to my boss and asked him if I could have two years worth of holidays all at once, which was the amount of time the tour would run.'

Jimmy's boss at the Shaftesbury Square estate agency, James McCartney, suggested that it was about time that he got this stage business out of his system for good. Years later, Jimmy recalled McCartney's words of advice to him:

"'I'll tell you what I'll do," he said. "You can't continue doing two jobs, both of which should be full time, at the same time. So I'll give you six weeks leave of absence from the firm with full pay. Go and do the tour and come back but remember, you won't get any more holidays for another two years."'

Jimmy was able to gain a great deal of experience in a variety of roles during his time with this company and he knew, in his heart of hearts, that this was the path he wanted to follow. He told McCartney that the theatre was going to be his full time career and, with that, he left behind his nine-to-five job forever to become a professional actor.

'As it turned out, I never did go back to the job of rent collector. Out of that six-week tour of Ulster, I was given what I suppose has been my most important break. A representative of an English management saw me and invited me to join a repertory theatre in Manchester. This, really, was the start of it all and I was terribly happy.'

The year was 1944 and a 26-year-old James Young left his beloved Northern Ireland for the first time to see what he could achieve across the water.

2

Jimmy's new boss was the Lancastrian impresario, Frank H Fortescue. A stalwart of the old time music hall scene, he now managed one of the most famous, not to mention successful, acting troupes in the country. Fortescue was a consummate showman and wily self-promoter, renowned for an occasional extravagance in the shows he staged. In 1941, for example, his production of *Cinderella* at the Theatre Royal in Worcester was hyped as including 'ponies, dogs and a goat from Gandy's circus'.

It was this penchant for attracting publicity for his shows that ensured that Fortescue's would be one of the last repertory companies to disappear from the travelling theatre circuit. Surviving well into the 1950s, the company maintained its popularity with a public desperate for distraction from the routine air raid warnings and rationing of the war years. A reliable source of entertainment, it also provided a beacon to people struggling to find their way amid the darkness and uncertainty that pervaded British society in the days after the war's end. Even the esteemed Shakespearean actor and film star, Sir Ian McKellen, admits to having fond memories of watching Fortescue's troupe perform.

By the time Jimmy had joined the Fortescue Players, they had taken up residence at the renowned Stockport Hippodrome, near Manchester. The Hippodrome itself was marked apart as a theatre of distinction. At the turn of the century, a certain Charles Chaplin had appeared on its stage – as the front end of a pantomime horse. Chaplin, of course, was to achieve global success as a master of silent cinema comedy, especially in his persona as the Little Tramp. It is probably not worth pondering too long, however, on the course of comedy history had Chaplin been asked to take the back end of that horse.

The combination of working for such a high profile repertory company at an important theatrical venue bode well for Jimmy's career. However, his initial experiences of arriving in England were less than glamorous.

'I arrived in Manchester on a Tuesday morning,' Jimmy remembered, 'and went straight along to the theatre with all my baggage. On the way, I saw posters advertising the first play that I would appear in, *If Four Walls Told.*'

The drama was a typically English affair, penned by Edward Percy, who enjoyed some success as a playwright but achieved international cult status as the wordsmith behind the 1960 Hammer horror, *The Brides of Dracula.* Billed as 'a village tale in three acts', it required Jimmy, in the role of Jan Rysing, to adopt a Cornish accent. Having 'no idea how Cornish people talked', he found that, by combining a northern and southern Irish accent, he could convince his English co-stars and audiences that he was speaking 'authentic Cornish, and it went very well'.

Jimmy was given his copy of the script and informed that rehearsals would start immediately as the first performance was scheduled for the following day.

After rehearsal, wandering around Manchester in search of somewhere to stay, Jimmy found it very difficult to get accommodation. Everywhere he went, he was told, 'We're full up.'

'Being both Irish and an actor is a considerable deterrent to any landlady but, eventually, I arrived at this sordid little cafe and they said they had a vacancy and took me up to a small room, at an extortionate rent, and left me in there with my suitcases.

'I took out the script and leafed through the 94 pages and thought, "How on earth am I going to learn half of this by tomorrow?"

'Then I opened the wardrobe to put a few things away and it fell apart and collapsed on me. It took me ages to get it back together and on its base again.

Jimmy as Edgar Linton in Wuthering Heights

'Those digs were very, very bad. On the third night, the landlady had left a little note for me to get my own supper, and I remember going into this sordid little kitchen and taking the lid off a saucepan to find a sort of stockpot. Around the edges of it was blue mould, which you would have to break to get at the liquid. This, of course, put me off not only my supper but also my food for the rest of the week.'

Jimmy was rescued from this life of squalor by a couple attached to the theatre. Their son was a stage manager who was away on tour and they asked Jimmy if he would like to live with them. He jumped at the chance and found himself looked after like a member of the family.

'They absolutely spoiled me. I would go

Jimmy with unidentified female co-star in The Patsy

Playing Danny the killer in Emlyn Williams' Night Must Fall

down in the mornings to find my socks turned inside out, ready to put on, and my shoes polished and laundry done. It was great.'

Appearing in over a hundred productions, Jimmy's *curriculum vitae* soon embraced an eclectic blend of high drama and lowbrow pantomime. Amid some lurid melodramas and engagements with Mother Goose, there were real highlights in the shape of Emily Brontë's *Wuthering Heights*, Rudolf Besier's *The Barretts of Wimpole Street*, *Love in a Mist* by Amelie Reeves and Gilbert Emery; and Barry Conner's *The Patsy*. While relishing his part in bringing such classics to a popular audience, Jimmy developed a particular fondness for the work of a playwright who was to become his literary hero at this juncture: Emlyn Williams.

Born in rural Wales in 1905, Williams was himself an accomplished actor as well as a writer. His thespian talents had led to many big screen appearances, including roles in projects as diverse as King Vidor's *The Citadel* and the last of Alfred Hitchcock's 1930s British classics, *Jamaica Inn*. Williams had even garnered the part of Caligula in Alexander Korda's overly ambitious and eventually abandoned production of *I, Claudius* in 1937. As a scribe, he had penned several screenplays – most notably *The Man Who Knew Too Much* (again for Hitchcock) in 1934 – and a host of key British plays of the period which achieved critical and commercial success. Among these plays were two which were to provide particularly good experiences for Jimmy.

'One of my favourites is his *Night Must Fall*, in which I played Danny, and what is almost an unknown thing for the repertory company happened: instead of running for one week, it ran for three.

'Afterwards, they sent me round several rep theatres owned by the same management, playing the part of Danny. They then put on a spate of Emlyn Williams, just for me, and one of the plays we did, which is still very dear to my heart, was *The Corn is Green*.'

Repertory theatre involved putting on a new play every week and placed great demands on the actors concerned. Over a typical seven days Jimmy, like his fellow rep actors, would be performing, committing to memory and rehearsing three scripts: the play being staged that particular week, the play being prepared for the following week, and a third play which was being produced the week after. A standard repertory production would have played to two houses nightly, so the combination of rehearsal and performance resulted in an exhausting workload.

In spite of this gruelling schedule, it provided fantastic training, augmenting Jimmy's natural talent as an actor and schooling him in the many facets of the theatre. He described the two years he spent in Manchester as 'wearying', while admitting to loving every minute of it.

'One week you would be doing modern comedy, the next a costume drama. Repertory theatre is a kind of factory that turns out plays relentlessly but it is a wonderful way to gain experience for a young actor.'

Staying with Fortescue for the two years straddling the end of conflict and the start of peacetime, Jimmy was able to contrast the changing make-up of audiences. By 1946, the guardians of the home front had given up their theatre seats to recently demobbed military personnel and a newly cynical general public, coming down after the unifying high of keeping home fires burning.

For reasons never made clear but which, possibly, could have been the result of Jimmy's desire for new horizons, he left Fortescue to join Harry Hanson's Players based in Aldershot. Unlike Fortescue's motley crew, these were actors who had the comparative luxury of performing only one show a night.

In 1946, Harry Hanson was in his late sixties but still saw himself as a man of about forty. His company had proved to be quite profitable for him and he was able to afford Saville Row suits to enhance his image. He was, however, completely bald and had bought himself two wigs to disguise the fact. Jimmy remembered:

'One was an iron-grey wig which he wore when he was in a good temper, and the other was an auburn wig, which he wore when he wasn't. If you ever saw him in the auburn wig, you scattered and got out of his way because you knew trouble was brewing.

'In order to add to this juvenile image that he had of himself, which certainly no one else had, he used to sprinkle a bit of salt on the collar of his dinner jacket to look like dandruff. This, incidentally, fooled nobody at all.'

Harry Hanson's Players was not a happy experience for Jimmy. The company was plagued by in-fighting and he soon decided that he would be better served looking for work elsewhere.

Naturally, he went to London, an hour's train journey from Aldershot, and wandered around the West End thinking how marvellous it would be to act there. Passing the New Theatre in Shaftesbury Avenue, he noticed a poster advertising an upcoming production of Sean O'Casey's classic *Red Roses For Me*.

Never one behind the door, Jimmy went to the box office and discovered that, while the play had been completely cast, the director was not fully satisfied with two of the parts. He was asked to leave his name and number and told that he would be contacted in case of recasting. Taking this as a polite rejection, Jimmy returned to Aldershot but was amazed when, two days later, he received a telegram asking him to report to the New Theatre that very day for an audition. He returned to London 'only to find a long, long queue of actors after the two parts'.

'We did read-throughs of the parts and, slowly, people were eliminated until there were only two of us left. We both waited, almost without breathing, for the decision and, amazingly, I was told I had got the job.'

The play ran for nearly seven months and Jimmy recalls that he 'felt on top of the world'. However, at the end of those seven months, he was unemployed once again.

It was then that he learned that his idol, Jimmy O'Dea, was auditioning for his new show, *Phil the Flutter's Ball*. The Ulsterman promptly showed up and, with his two years of repertory experience standing him in good stead, managed to join the cast.

Among the other actors who joined the show around this time was Violet Carson, who would one day play hair-netted battleaxe, Ena Sharples, in the long running soap opera, *Coronation Street*.

Phil the Flutter's Ball was an instant success and James Young's London career seemed set, at least for the foreseeable future. Unfortunately, one night, fate stepped in and determined to cut short Jimmy's happiness in working with O'Dea.

'I was performing in a sketch, during which some members of the audience were invited on stage to participate. Somehow, things got out of hand and I accidentally managed to hurt one gentleman and totally ruin his clothes. Witnessing this, the English audience became quite irate and started to boo and jeer me unmercifully. The gentleman in question complained bitterly to the management, threatening them with a lawsuit and, as a consequence, I was given the sack. Needless to say, I was heartbroken and came very close to giving up the theatre for good.'

Out of work once again, a depressed and dejected Jimmy decided that it might not be a bad idea to get away from London for a while. While scanning the advertisements in the theatrical trade publication, *The Stage*, he noticed that a company was looking for actors to go on a tour of the

Danny makes his entrance

Middle East in two Welsh productions. Jimmy was immediately interested as one of the plays was his beloved *Night Must Fall*.

The tour was being arranged under the auspices of Combined Services Entertainment, an organisation which had replaced the Entertainments National Service Association (or ENSA, as it was more popularly known) at the end of the war.

Jimmy later explained that 'companies were

going all over the globe to places where British soldiers, starved of their own type of entertainment, were in occupation. The tour was scheduled for two years but I wasn't perturbed at that. News of the long stint in a faraway place decimated the number of actors looking for the part but there were still about a hundred in the running when I was auditioned.'

The auditions were held at the Whitehall Theatre, which would become a household name to many because of the celebrated Whitehall Farces staged there from 1947 until 1969 by comic actor, Brian Rix. Jimmy turned up, discovering that he was the only Irishman among a host of hopeful Welsh actors.

'I went along and queued up four flights of stairs on which, I think, was every Welsh actor in the British Isles … I kept my mouth shut because I thought I would be eliminated before I ever got into the audition with my accent.

'But I got through the first read-through and was told come back the next day. I got through the second read-through and was successful again. There were a total of four read-throughs until, finally, there were just four of us left. I must say, at that point, I was delighted to have got as far as I had.'

To everyone's amazement, Jimmy beat the other Welsh actors for the part and, after a scant two weeks rehearsal, he found himself on his way to the Middle East. It was on 5 July 1946 that Jimmy and the troupe arrived in Egypt.

'We landed in Cairo and, as soon as I saw the place, I regretted my decision. It was roasting, there were flies everywhere, and you only had to appear in the street and a dozen urchins would crowd around like insects, trying to sell you everything from a dirty postcard to their big sister. But, somehow, I grew to like the idea and thoroughly enjoyed the whole thing after a few short weeks.'

Jimmy in Palestine

The local army high command, which was given responsibility for the actors, decided that they should initially be billeted inside the divisional headquarters instead of a local civilian hotel. This was for their own protection as it was felt they would not be safe due to the current state of unrest in the country. It was a very dangerous time to arrive in the Middle East as terrorists were targeting British personnel across the country. On 26 July 1946, shortly after Jimmy and his troupe had arrived, members of the Jewish terrorist organisation, *Irgun Tsvai-Leumi*, planted and exploded a bomb at the King David Hotel in Jerusalem. The hotel was the base for the British Military Command and the British Criminal Investigation Division. 91 people were killed, 28 of them British.

Jimmy and the company toured all over Egypt and Israel in R F

The Combined Services Entertainment troupe. The girl on the left is Liz, Jimmy's one-time fiancee

Delderfield's comedy, *Worm's Eye View*. Whilst on the road, Jimmy became close to a girl in the company named Liz. Although virtually nothing is known about the relationship, or the girl, they were so enamoured of each other that they got engaged. The union clearly didn't last, however, as it was during this part of the tour that Jimmy first encountered the person who was to become inextricably linked with his career, and his personal life, for the next three decades.

After one of the shows, the cast was invited back for a meal at the mess of the Cheshire Regiment. As Jimmy walked into the hall, he saw a very tall, slim young man, sitting at the table with a glass in his hand. The young man got up as Jimmy came through the door, walked over, and extended his hand.

'I enjoyed your performance enormously,' he said. 'Good evening, my name is Jack Hudson.'

Jack had been born in London in 1923, living what seems to be an uneventful life. At the age of 19, he had gone straight from school into the fold of the military where, as a model soldier, he had climbed up the ranks in tune with the progress of the war. Now, as Captain, he was put in charge of the actors' troupe, taking care of their every need during their stay in the Middle East. He and Jimmy hit it off immediately, heralding the start of a beautiful friendship. Jimmy reminisced:

'No matter where we went, either in the deserts of Egypt or in hostile Palestine, the Captain would see to it that we were excellently housed and courteously treated. His efficiency and administrative ability were remarkable and I resolved that, if I ever were in a position to organise my own productions back home, he would be just the man to partner me.'

Jimmy relaxing backstage at Port Said between rehearsals

After the tour with *Worm's Eye View* had finished, the company returned to their base in the region, at Port Said, on the northern end of the Suez Canal, to rehearse for *Night Must Fall*. When this opened at the Cairo Opera House, the great and the good were there to see it. Even King Farouk of Egypt graced opening night with his presence.

'It was a glorious first night,' enthused Jimmy, 'with all this glamour, except that towards the end of the play, where Danny is arrested and the detective clamps handcuffs over his wrist, the actor playing the detective was so excited that he caught my wrist in the handcuffs. I had to play my last, very pathetic speech with blood pouring out everywhere. I thought I was going to faint.'

Away from the smell of the greasepaint, Jimmy and the

other cast members occasionally sought relaxation at some of the nearby beauty spots. One day, they were visiting a beach for a spot of swimming. After they arrived, some menacing looking locals started threatening them. They kept spitting on the ground and mumbling, 'Feelthy Breetesh'. One of the men then pulled out a dagger and things began to look very nasty. Luckily, Jimmy saved the day when he replied, in his own Ulster accent, 'Look fellas, we're Irish.' The locals broke into broad smiles and offered handshakes all round saying, 'Ah, so you've had your troubles with the Breetesh peegs as well!'

Jack Hudson had problems of a different nature to contend with, as he later pointed out.

'When I arrived in Haifa with my ship, I had to organise the disembarkation of the soldiers and the off-loading of supplies. The dock was total bedlam, with street urchins running up to the soldiers and shouting, "Would you like to have a good time? Come and I will take you to meet my sister, very pretty girl, very reasonable."

"I was having a lot of trouble getting things organised and, when one of these boys ran up to me, I said, "I'm not interested in your sister. I want the Harbour Master."

'The boy looked up at me and, perfectly seriously, said, "Well sir, that will cost a little bit extra."

'Another time, two soldiers under my command were involved in a road traffic accident with a civilian car outside the barracks. As per the army regulations, they had to file a report stating the circumstances surrounding the crash. I read their report the next day and couldn't believe what they had written.

Lieutenant Jack Hudson

'"While returning to base yesterday," they wrote, "our jeep was involved in a collision with a civilian vehicle. When we got out and approached the other car, we discovered the occupants were two wogs."

'I was horrified at such racism and called them in immediately. I said to them, "That report is an absolute disgrace. Do you know that one of the occupants of the car you hit was King Farouk of Egypt? Go and rewrite it and have it back on my desk in an hour."

'An hour later, the report arrived back with me and I had a look through it again. It now read, "While returning to base yesterday, our jeep was involved in a collision with a civilian vehicle. When we got out and approached the other car, we discovered the occupants were King Farouk – and another wog."

At the end of Jimmy's contract with Combined Service Entertainment, he returned to England. Jack, who had been demobbed just shortly beforehand, was there to greet him when his boat docked in Liverpool.

Jimmy had hoped to get back into his old repertory company in Manchester but found that he was not required. He did the rounds of several local reps but his heart really wasn't in it.

'I went along to Oldham repertory and looked at the town and, after the glorious sunshine of the Middle East and my nostalgic memories of Northern Ireland, I thought, "This is not for me." At the same time, Jack looked around smoky, wet Manchester and said, "Well, I don't think this is for me either."'

Jimmy wanted to return to his native city to see his family again after being away for so long. Without further ado, he booked himself a passage home and Jack agreed to follow him over.

'It was a long, long time since I had heard a Northern Ireland accent, and I can remember, from the next cabin, there floated out this gorgeous Irish voice which said, "Hay steward, how much is the tea?"'

'And the steward answered, "Sixpence a cup, sir."'

'So the Belfast voice said, "Right, bring us two cups and I'll square ye up in the morning."'

'I could have rushed in and kissed them because it was a gorgeous sound and I hadn't heard it for years.'

Jimmy was ecstatic to be back home and, as soon as Jack joined him, they moved into a flat over Johnston's butcher's shop on the Newtownards Road in east Belfast. They started to plan what they would do next. In Palestine, they had often spoken about how great it would be to work together in the theatre and they had hoped to get something organised right away. However, as Jimmy remembered it:

'My arrival back in Belfast was greeted by an unstifled yawn from all the people who should have sat up and taken notice at the plans I had made. But it was different then … and the post-war boom in the world of the theatre was grinding to a halt. There didn't seem to be much room for new ideas and a fresh approach. After talking to just about everybody in the business, it seemed that the hours that Jack and I had spent in enthusiastic chat had been time wasted.'

Jimmy returned to his old stomping ground, the Group Theatre, which was still under the management of Harold Goldblatt and the other directors. The first play he starred in on his return was George Bernard Shaw's *Candida*. His co-star was the doyenne of Irish theatre, Margaret D'Arcy, who personified grace, style and professionalism. D'Arcy would later refer to Jimmy's portrayal of Eugene, the 'wild, imaginative poet' as being 'very, very good'. As usual, the Group management was not overly generous with the salary and Jimmy was working six days a week for just ninety bob (about £4.50).

Jack found employment as the manager of the famous Plaza Ballroom in Chichester Street, Belfast, but his position there was short lived. Subsequently, he became an investigator with the National Assistance Board, checking the validity of claims by people seeking financial support from the government.

It seemed that the idea of working together in the theatre would never come to fruition and the pair became so depressed with the situation that they were actually on the brink of emigrating to Australia to start a new life together. They wrote off to Australia and got in touch with a broadcasting station in Sydney. The owners of the station told them that, while they could not promise them a concrete position, there would, more than likely, be work for them once they came over.

'The ravaged, war torn city of Belfast I had left was already being rebuilt,' Jimmy later said. 'There was a tremendous air of optimism underlying the superficial gloom caused by food rationing and all the other necessary evils that follow total war. That optimism, that urge, to recreate something vital from the ashes, hadn't penetrated very far into the world of Ulster theatre.

'I had come back and found the living theatre here dominated by the same people, the same plays and the same attitudes I had left four years before. There didn't seem to be much in it for me so, after playing a couple of months in the Group Theatre for ninety bob a week, I booked a sailing ticket to Australia ... I was never to take up that booking for, within a couple of weeks of the departure date something happened that was change my whole future dramatically.'

And it was all to change with a little assistance from a window cleaner called Derek.

Arty by Millar and Mageean: one of Jimmy's many appearances at the Group on his return from the Middle East

THE ULSTER GROUP THEATRE

Present,

A LIGHT COMEDY IN THREE ACTS

by RUDDICK MILLAR
and JAMES MAGEEAN

"ARTY"

JAMES YOUNG
as
"ARTY"

3

When Joseph Tomelty was approached by BBC Northern Ireland producer, John Boyd, to write a programme focussing on an everyday working-class Belfast family, the seeds were sown for the most popular radio serial in local broadcasting history.

Tomelty, who was born in the County Down village of Portaferry in 1911, had written some key productions for the Group Theatre. These included *Barnum Was Right* and *Right Again, Barnum*, the latter of which had been an important stepping stone in Jimmy's theatrical career. He later wrote a masterpiece of the Irish theatre in the form of *All Souls' Night*, as well as two fine novels, *Red is the Port Light* and *The Apprentice*.

Tomelty helped to further cement the Group's reputation as a source of excellent drama with his masterful performances in St John Ervine's *Boyd's Shop* and his own projects, *Is the Priest at Home?* and *Highly Efficient*. His presence on the stage was later summarised by actor and writer John Keyes: 'Joseph Tomelty, cast well, was a magnificent actor. But it was always too easy for Joe. His personality was magnetic, his talents deep and various. He commanded a stage simply by being on it. It seemed no effort at all.'

It was this magnetism which brought Tomelty to the attention of filmmakers, who utilised his talents to memorable effect in *Hobson's Choice* (1954), alongside Charles Laughton, *Moby Dick* (1956) and *A Night to Remember* (1958). While filming *Bhowani Junction* with Ava Gardner in 1954, he had a car accident which brought his writing and acting virtually to a halt. The occasional appearance on screen would follow but, by this time, Tomelty's golden years were prematurely behind him.

All this, however, was to come. When Tomelty accepted that BBC commission, he set about fashioning a show based on the successful Scottish radio hit, *The*

Joseph Tomelty, the creative force behind the McCooeys

The First Family of Northern Ireland: The McCooeys, *the most popular local radio serial ever broadcast*

The series proved so popular that the Cityweek *newspaper printed a cartoon strip based on the characters every week*

McFlannels, which featured Molly Weir – in her pre-*Flash* floor cleaning days – and centred on a family of working class Glaswegians. The result was *The McCooeys*.

The title of the show was settled on after Tomelty had checked the local telephone directory to ensure that the name of the eponymous family was not listed in an effort to avoid any accusation of religious bias.

Featuring many of Tomelty's associates from the Group, including J G Devlin and Elizabeth Begley, *The McCooeys* premiered on 13 May 1949. From the very beginning, with the strains of the street song *My Aunt Jane* as its signature tune, the show was a crowd puller. Pioneering in its use of local vernacular, the action centred on the exploits of the McCooey family as related to the audience by the family grocer, Bobby Greer, played by Tomelty himself. In an era before television, the streets of Belfast would empty every Saturday evening between 6.20 and 6.40 as people rushed home to huddle by their radio sets and listen to the show. Some observed that, during those 20 minutes, a murder could have been committed and nobody would know a thing about it until the programme was over.

The recognisable cast of characters included Sammy and Maggie McCooey who, with their children, Sally, Meta and Willy, and Sammy's father, known simply as Grandda, were to become household favourites over the show's seven year life. In fact, *The McCooeys* proved so popular that the entertainment newspaper, *Cityweek*, regularly devoted a whole page to a comic strip version.

As Bobby Greer waxed lyrically about 'shloup with vegabittles' and characters responded to various witticisms with 'You're a comeejan', the show soon became very much a part of the Saturday evening routine. Some listeners got so involved in the characters and storylines that, when the McCooey family redecorated their parlour, many phoned the BBC to express alarm that they hadn't fixed a price for the work beforehand. Others suggested a rate that would be best suited to the job required.

Jimmy in his late twenties

When Tomelty decided to introduce a new character to the show, based loosely on Willie John from *Right Again, Barnum*, he turned to Jimmy who had made that part his own several years earlier. Tomelty's collaborations with Jimmy had proved particularly fruitful, as had recently been demonstrated when he played Lenny to Jimmy's George in a critically acclaimed 1948 Group production of John Steinbeck's *Of Mice and Men*. John Keyes declared later that 'James Young gave the performance of his life.'

Jimmy also received kudos for his part as Stephen Quinn in Tomelty's *All Souls' Night*, prompting Keyes to observe that it 'made one ever after regret his desertion of the legitimate theatre.'

Jimmy's character in *The McCooeys* was devised as a slightly camp window cleaner called Derek. He recalled the public response after Derek made his debut on the show.

'It started off only as a bit part really but, within five weeks, it had developed considerably. The main reason was the fact that a lot of people had taken time to write to the BBC saying how much they enjoyed the character.

'After the second or so broadcast, the national papers started coming to interview me at the Group Theatre where I was appearing every night for less than £5 a week. But, at this stage, Jack and I still had our tickets booked for Australia. Then, one day, the BBC head of programmes, Henry McMullen, called me into his office and said that, if he guaranteed me three broadcasts out of four on *The McCooeys*, would I be willing to stay.

Jimmy meets a real life Derek at Belfast's Broadcasting House

THE 100TH EDITION OF

'THE
McCOOEYS'

The story of a Belfast family
Written by
JOSEPH TOMELTY

Produced by
SAM DENTON

AT 7.25

*Marking the
100th episode of
The McCooeys*

'The only reason I had thought of going to Australia was for more money. This was enough to make me cancel the ticket. I was now getting £20 a broadcast from the BBC for *The McCooeys* plus my £5 a week at the Group.'

John Keyes remembers that, immediately after Jimmy's first appearance as Derek, his 'catch phrases were on the mouths of every schoolboy and schoolgirl in Belfast.'

Incredibly, Jimmy only performed on five episodes of *The McCooeys* but he made such a lasting impact that, even to this day, his name is steadfastly linked with the show. Commenting on the classic radio serial years later, Jimmy recalled that, after his fifth episode, McMullen took him aside and informed him that 'the author says he cannot write any more parts for Derek the window cleaner.' Jimmy was to describe this blow as 'the greatest disappointment of my life up to that point.'

He had his own theory about why one of the most popular characters was being dropped.

'After five appearances in *The McCooeys*, Derek was no longer featured. Why? Well, when I arrived back after a few years across the water, the "oul hands" here thought that I was a bit uppity. Not that I was I hope. It was just that they expected it. When I arrived backstage at the Group at rehearsal time, there would be murmurs of "Oh, here comes the star, now we can begin", and that sort of thing. I didn't let it worry me, mainly because I had served my apprenticeship in the tough school of English provincial repertory, where catty comments flew about the auditorium 12 hours a day.'

At the time, there was a big outcry from listeners for the return of Derek but he was never brought back.

However, the success of the radio show had already had a great knock-on effect on the bookings for the Group. People who had never ever been to the theatre began buying tickets to see 'Derek', despite the fact that Jimmy was playing a completely different character in the current play. Although Jimmy's time as a radio star had seemingly come to an abrupt end, he had captured the public's imagination. James Young was now a household name and everyone wanted to see him perform.

Hoping to capitalise on his positive influence on the Group's box office, Jimmy went to the management of the theatre and asked for another £1 a week. However, they refused, arguing that it was a very small theatre and they couldn't afford to increase his pay.

By this stage, Jimmy was receiving better offers from elsewhere.

'At this time, promoters of concerts were coming to me and asking me just to walk on their stage … offering me £20 or £30 or £40. Each time, though, I turned them down. Eventually, a promoter came to me and said we will give you £150 for three appearances at St Mary's Hall, Belfast.'

As Jimmy and Jack Hudson had talked about eventually setting up their own production company, the financial advantage of the St Mary's Hall performances was obvious. Throwing together a short script with a running time of 14 minutes which, by Jack's admission, was 'absolutely awful', the pair planned what was to be Jimmy's first stand-up variety spot.

'Oh now.' Jimmy as Derek the window cleaner

On his opening night at St Mary's, he walked out to a full house and received a rapturous welcome. Frozen with fear about appearing alone on stage, he tried to start the show but found he couldn't get any words out. Luckily, the audience continued applauding, allowing him to compose himself again. As the clamour died down, he uttered the two words which had become his catch phrase during his short run on *The McCooeys*: 'Oh now.'

In later years, Jack described the impact of those two little words on the assembled crowd.

'How improbable those two words look in print, how meaningless. There is no way I can reproduce the impact of the words as he delivered them, the upward inflection of the voice, the facial expression, the manner of meaning that they conveyed. If you are not Irish, or do not know the mentality behind the phrase, it is completely devoid of significance, but that audience was ready for it.'

The catch phrase brought the house down again and gave him his first laugh of the evening.

Brimming with confidence now, he carried on with the rest of the act and had the audience rolling in the aisles for the whole show which, due to some quick ad-libbing, finally stretched to a length of 38 minutes. Jack noted down as many of the ad-libs as he could and they became part of the subsequent shows. This was a process of script development that Jimmy would continue to use throughout his career.

As the nights went on, the act expanded until it had a running time of 45 minutes. By the end of the engagement at St Mary's, the pair had earned the equivalent of 21 weeks at the Group Theatre.

Spurred on by the success of their first real enterprise together, Jimmy and Jack decided to accept more engagements from around the country, establishing James Young Productions in the process.

'After the show in St Mary's Hall, on Jack's suggestion, I got a company together and toured Northern Ireland, appearing in town halls and theatres. This, I suppose, was really the start of the James Young and Jack Hudson business partnership. He booked all the halls, arranged all the transport and looked after the accounts side of the business.'

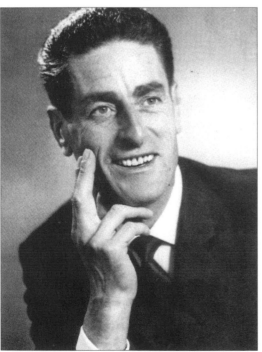

Taking care of business: Jack Hudson

Ivan Martin, the popular Downtown Radio presenter, who served his acting apprenticeship under Jimmy's tutelage in the 1960s, elaborates on the business relationship between Jimmy and Jack.

'If it hadn't been for Jack, Jimmy's business life would have been in complete disarray. Jimmy was far too generous, too kind and totally disinterested in things like figures. Jack looked after the business side of the theatre and looked after it very well. He was very adept at that.'

The partners soon realised that a bit of variety was required if they wished to entertain an audience for a whole evening. Jimmy also needed the opportunity to change costumes between comedy skits. The first thing they required was some musical accompaniment and, with this in mind, Jimmy enlisted the aid of a gifted musician named Tommy James.

'I needed a pianist for the show and heard about Tommy, so I went along to see him. In those days, he was running a small record shop on the Grosvenor Road. I heard him play and booked him. Tommy was a very excellent musician and, later, when we were in the Empire Theatre ... he became a fantastic musical director. He conducted the orchestra, did all the arrangements and was a most efficient person, someone for whom I have a very great affection.'

Tommy James later became a household name in Northern Ireland with his own Ulster Television show, *Teatime with Tommy*.

He was their only means of music in those early days and had to provide the backing for the show using the piano or organ supplied by the venue. The instrument was often in a very poor state of repair and out of tune, but Jack recounted that 'Tommy would run his fingers up and down the keys and say, "Bloody awful, isn't it?" and then manage to make it sound like a Steinway Grand.'

A bit of glamour was added to the show with the female dance duo, Melda and Molly Davey. Melda was also a natural comedienne and was to become one of the usual suspects appearing alongside Jimmy in his 1960s Group farces.

The format of the shows was very much like the old music hall variety performances Jimmy enjoyed in his younger days. Drawing on his memories of watching Jimmy O'Dea on the stage of the Empire, he set about creating a similar showcase for himself.

Jimmy, the enterprising showman behind James Young Productions

The backbone of the show would be a series of skits featuring Jimmy, with the occasional assistance of Jack. These would be interspersed with musical numbers, the playing of Tommy James and the surefooted rhythms of the Davey sisters. If a local tenor or soprano were available, he or she would be booked to bring a touch of class to the evening.

The James Young travelling revue toured the towns and cities of the north in an old station wagon, procured by Jimmy for £200. Whether it was Markethill, Newry or Derry, Jimmy was always impressed by the 'long queues outside the theatre. This tour got us financially on a firm footing, which was fortunate, as I had used up all my money in buying the station wagon.'

The response from the audiences was tremendous and the earlier idea of pursuing a new life and career elsewhere was soon forgotten.

'We were doing revue with the company and this felt a bit strange as I had been brought up in the straight theatre. It is a different form of entertainment, but I enjoyed doing it very much. Jack told me he thought that, as we were doing so well, it would be foolish to think of leaving Northern Ireland for Australia or anywhere else.'

One of their favourite dates was the town hall in Limavady because of the guaranteed enthusiastic welcome. The one problem with the venue was the design of the stage. The back curtain was right against the theatre wall and the wings did not lead to an exit. As a result of this, the performers could not discreetly get from one side of the stage to the other during the performance and props, which had not been placed at the correct side of the stage at the start of the show, could not be used.

Jimmy also had a thing about not being seen by the audience before the show, feeling that his initial appearance added to the magic of the evening. However, there was no access to the stage except through the audience and, to keep out of sight, he often had to remain in the small wing space off and on from 6pm until 11.30pm – the time the second house let out. Even by attempting to use the toilet between shows, Jimmy risked being spotted by a member of the public, so the entire evening became an endurance test on his bladder. He would often joke to friends: 'If you want to develop strong kidneys try playing Limavady a few times.'

In the summer of 1950, Jimmy was asked to perform at a beauty contest at the Pickie Pool in Bangor, County Down. Just as he had started his act, a woman got up from her seat and started making her way down the centre aisle towards him. He stopped talking and watched her as she made her way to one of the side exits, obviously on her way to the toilets.

'I didn't think I was that bad,' he shouted after her. 'Anyway, give me a chance, missus, I've hardly started!'

The audience burst into fits of laughter and the poor woman quickly sought refuge in the toilets. As the door to the toilets closed behind her, Jimmy continued, 'Mention my name and they'll give you a good seat.'

Quickly realising the comic potential of the situation, Jimmy put aside his rehearsed script and ad-libbed further to the woman's embarrassment and the audience's delight. 'Now you mustn't laugh at the poor woman. It might happen to you one day.'

While the woman was returning to her seat, the onslaught continued: 'Anyway, I'll not start until she gets back or she'll be forever wondering what I was talking about. Ah, there she is… Do you feel better now, missus? That's right, make room for her, make way there.'

In the end, Jimmy milked more laughs out of the lady going off to the lavatory than from his prepared act and the event ran 15 minutes over schedule.

*The Legion
Hall in Bangor,
rechristened the
Legion Theatre
by Jimmy and
Jack*

This incident would form the template for a feature of Jimmy's future
live performances. It always worked particularly well in small theatres with
people who arrived late or had to go out for some reason. By moving to
and from their seats, they would become fair game for Jimmy and his
barbed comments, leading to such classic put downs as, 'Isn't that a
beautiful coat? I wonder if that style will ever come back.'

The summer season had the reputation as being a notoriously bad time
for touring provincial towns. So, in 1951, Jimmy arranged to rent the
British Legion Hall in Bangor as a fixed base for presenting a revue show
over the holiday period.

'Jack told me that he thought there must be a market for a summer
season and I have always had a very great affection for Bangor because that
was the place where, as a kid in short trousers, I stood through three
performances a day of the open-air concert party.

'Mind you, everyone thought we were mad to consider doing a summer season there. Whenever they heard we were going, they all threw their eyes up to the ceiling and said, "Bangor is a showman's graveyard because no one in history has ever been known to make money there in the summer. People there just don't go to shows then." However, Jack Hudson had a very shrewd business sense and I trusted him implicitly. He leased the Legion Hall and we rechristened it the Legion Theatre.'

The Bangor shows brought out the creative side of Jack, who transformed the stage of the Legion Theatre with ten sets of colourful curtains and over a mile of bunting which he had laboriously made on an old Singer sewing machine. His role as stage and prop designer for Jimmy's shows would continue for the next two decades.

On the first Monday in July 1951, the Bangor revue opened. Despite the warnings of the nay-sayers, Jimmy reported that the house was 'packed at every possible performance. In the end, I was to play there for nine consecutive years in what were probably some of the most successful summer seasons held anywhere.'

Indeed, some members of the audience became such keen fans of Jimmy that they came back for more. One example of this was the Bangor couple, Mr and Mrs Foster Davidson, who were to permanently book the same seats at Jimmy's show – Row B, Seats 8 and 9 – for the next nine years!

Every day, Jimmy and Jack arrived at 11am to open the box office. This was followed by a visit to the local florists on Hamilton Road. The proprietor, Miss Forde, supplied the flowers with which Jimmy would lovingly create magnificent displays for the foyer. To him, these displays were an important feature of the theatre's appearance.

George Lodge,
manager of the
Grand Opera House

The two business partners manned the box office in shifts while other members of the company took care of any odd jobs around the theatre. A small bed, used in some of the sketches, was stored at the back of the stage

and put to good use when Jimmy or Jack had to catch up on some much needed sleep in the afternoon.

During the Bangor run, Jimmy was to encounter J Ritchie McKee for the first time. An estate agent by profession, McKee was one of the wealthiest and most influential men in the province. His many roles included Governor of the BBC and Chairman of the Council for Encouragement of Music and the Arts (CEMA), a precursor to the Arts Council of Northern Ireland. He was also the Chairman of the Group Theatre's Board of Directors. Visiting Jimmy backstage after a performance, McKee remarked that the show had been 'one of the most pleasant evenings' he had ever had in his life. This was to be the start of a friendship that would have important consequences for Jimmy's later career.

The only hiccup in running the Legion Theatre occurred on Wednesday mornings when the building was used as the local Petty Sessions Court. The brightly decorated theatre provided an unlikely backdrop for matters of the law but the local judiciary did not seem to mind. Every Wednesday, the stage curtain would be lowered and the seats reorganised. The Resident Magistrate would enter the building and say to Jimmy, 'Good morning, James. I hope your business is as good as mine today.'

The Bangor summer season proved to be a very profitable venture for James Young Productions with full houses for every performance. It showed that there was a large audience for Jimmy's brand of comedy and it was now time to expand on it.

'Jack Hudson came to me and said that I shouldn't be playing in small halls but in places like the Opera House. So Jack went along to the Opera House to see the owner, a very wonderful man called George Lodge.'

Jack asked Lodge if he was interested in staging a James Young show for one week and was amazed at the reply.

'I'm sorry,' Lodge told Jack, 'but (Jimmy) didn't accept my terms when I offered it to him before, and then he went and appeared in St. Mary's Hall. I don't look down on St. Mary's Hall but I cannot charge Opera House prices for someone who is sort of second hand.'

Jack replied that Jimmy had never had any offer to appear at the Grand Opera House, prompting Lodge to explain that he had approached Jimmy through the management of the Group. He had told them that he'd wanted Jimmy to top the bill for one week but, when he went back for an answer, he'd been informed that Jimmy was frightened of variety and wouldn't do it at any price. Jimmy spoke of his shock.

Jimmy with Patrick Alinney in Tyrone Guthrie's production of The Passing Day, *staged especially for the Festival of Britain*

'It turned out he had offered £500 for that one week. I had never been told by anyone at the Group that this offer had been made and when Jack came back and told me I cried for two days. My big ambition had been to play top of the bill in the theatre where, a few years before, I had sat in the prompter's corner for ten bob a week. But George Lodge was a kind man and he told Jack if I ever made a big impact on radio again he would think about it.'

Meanwhile, back at BBC Broadcasting House, Jimmy's growing success on the variety circuit had not gone unnoticed. Henry McMullen approached Jimmy and Jack and asked if they could devise a show that would include music and comedy sketches. McMullen admitted to being impressed by Jimmy's ability to 'play a big variety of different characters'.

'Why not try and sandwich all these characters you can play from your observations of Belfast people into a programme?' asked McMullen. 'If you can do this and find a suitable scriptwriter, I am willing to give you half an hour a week and we will call it *The James Young Show*.'

While hammering out ideas for his radio series, Jimmy was invited by Tyrone Guthrie, one of the foremost theatre directors of the twentieth century, to join the company of actors he had rallied together to perform at the Festival of Britain. Some of the other local talent involved included old comrades, Joseph Tomelty and Patrick McAlinney, from the Group. Jimmy was very flattered and accepted immediately.

When Guthrie revived Ballymoney playwright George Shiels' 1936 play, *The Passing Day*, at the Ambassador Theatre in London, Jimmy was cast in the lead role. His portrayal of the miserly merchant garnered him high praise and provided a reminder to those who needed reminding of his credentials as a fine dramatic actor.

However, Jimmy had little time to savour his success since the BBC in Northern Ireland were anxious that the planned radio series should materialise. Eventually, a meeting was called to bring together potential scriptwriters and Jimmy flew home to attend it.

'We got home and went to the meeting, which seemed to be packed with every scriptwriter and would-be scriptwriter Northern Ireland ever had. They were all wringing their hands and saying, "This is money for jam". They didn't realise just how difficult writing comedy for radio really is. In fact I later had a letter from Henry saying that out of all the people who had attended the meeting only three scripts had materialised, two of which were unworkable technically and badly constructed and the third was so dirty that it couldn't possibly be used on the air.'

Jimmy and Jack turned to Michael Bishop, who had worked with a number of British comedians. He was a good technical writer but had never seen Belfast in his life and, being English, could not understand the dialect or the characters. Nevertheless, he managed to produce a satisfactory script, which Jimmy embellished with some localisms. When it was sent to Henry McMullen, the BBC immediately commissioned another three on the strength of it.

It was time for James Young's return to radio, this time in his very own show.

4

When the first episode of Jimmy's live 1951 radio show, *The Young Idea*, was broadcast, it was clear that the BBC had surrounded their comic wonder-boy with some exceptional local talent. Amongst the cast were Patrick McAlinney and John F Tyrone, both Group veterans, and both actors of real talent.

McAlinney, who hailed from Omagh, was a veteran of the early days of the Group, continually impressing in the exceptional productions staged at the Belfast theatre. A star actor there, he went on to portray a gallery of Irish policemen, barmen and clergymen in film and television projects as diverse as *Shake Hands with the Devil*, *The Omen* and *The Liver Birds*. These unchallenging assignments on screen betrayed a respectable theatre career that embraced a personal triumph with his involvement with the Theatre Royal, Haymarket's staging of *The Matchmaker*. This 1954 production of Thornton Wilder's period comedy was to transfer successfully to Broadway the following year, with McAlinney intact.

John F Tyrone, on the other hand, was to find his career closely linked with Jimmy's in the days following that first radio episode. Tyrone had helped establish the Group Theatre and was a member of its original board of directors. Before the acting bug was permitted to bite too deeply, he had been a Belfast solicitor under his real name, John Moss. His involvement in Jimmy's future radio and stage work was to raise his profile considerably

Patricia Stewart and Jimmy in rehearsal

as a local celebrity. However, some commentators considered this involvement to be seriously at odds with his earlier thespian roots. John Keyes notes wryly that Tyrone 'made an easy transition and acted – I use that word loosely – for James Young without, apparently, feeling that he was, in any way, letting the side down.'

Nevertheless, both McAlinney and Tyrone – in the company of Bridie Ward, Patricia Stewart, Frank J Murphy and Noel Lloyd – should be commended for the part they played, whether as sidekicks or foils, in ensuring that Jimmy's series was a success.

To all intents and purposes a carbon copy of his travelling variety shows and Bangor summer seasons, *The Young Idea* brought Jimmy's brand of observational comedy to a wider audience. As well as topical material, Jimmy introduced his listeners to characters that were to become familiar friends. These included Wee Sammy the schoolboy; Big Aggie's man, the slightly inebriated shipyard worker; and, of course, Mrs O'Condriac, who would attend the doctor's surgery every week without fail, except for the odd time when she couldn't go – because she wasn't well! Then there was the Cherryvalley snob, of whom Jack Hudson was to write:

'With her grossly affected accent, she always saw herself as being better than her peers and always putting one over on them. When asked about the rates in Cherryvalley she would reply, "Oh, we have no rates in Cherryvalley. No *rates*, only mice!

'And when she met an old friend she had not seen for some time, she would say, "I wouldn't have known a bit of you! You've grown so old. It must be years and years since I last seen you. I wouldn't have known you only for your coat!"'

Providing the musical interludes on the show was a Dublin group called The Four Ramblers. The lead singer was Val Doonican. Later to claim that he was one of those acts who had taken years to become famous overnight, Val was to host his own television series, crooning easy listening tunes to millions of Saturday evening viewers in the 70s. On Jimmy's show, he was positively baby-faced and had a long way to go before popularising V-necked sweaters and rocking chairs to the extent that he eventually did.

To round things off, Tommy James' gentle tinkling on the ivories was replaced by the full-blown backing of the BBC Northern Light Orchestra, under the baton of David Curry.

The Young Idea became a great success and spawned further series over the ensuing years such as *Young's Way, Young and Foolish, Young Again* and

Recording The Young Idea *at the Empire Theatre in Belfast*

Jimmy with Patrick McAlinney and Bridie Ward in The Young Idea

Great to be Young. Jimmy was able to test comedy material on a live audience during his Bangor summer season and fine tune it before it was used on the shows recorded in the autumn.

These shows, by Jimmy's own admission, raised his profile immeasurably, bringing him recognition 'sometimes from the most unlikely places'. He was later to tell of an incident that occurred while on holiday in Spain. He was talking to a friend in a hotel when an English couple approached him.

'They came over from their table and asked if they'd met me somewhere before. It turned out that they recognised my voice from the programme all those years before. Needless to say, I was very flattered.'

He also enlisted the help of two young Scottish writers named John Law and Bill Craig to work on the scripts for the show. This talented duo found the experience an invaluable grounding for their later successes, which included writing for such popular comedians as Arthur Haynes and Tony Hancock.

After two years, the management of the Empire Theatre asked Jimmy to develop his radio formula into a live variety revue for them.

'We were very pleased when the manager, Frank Reynolds, came and asked me if we would do a season there. Apart from the fact that it was a very good showplace, there were sentimental reasons why I had always

James Young in
'YOUNG'S WAY'

On Friday the Ulster comedian
presents some old friends and new
acquaintances from his collection
of the characters whom he meets in
a city street (see page 9)

*Radio Times cover
picture for Jimmy's
radio series,* Young's
Way

wanted to appear there. It was the first theatre I had visited as a kid and
the place I had watched Jimmy O'Dea, who was my great idol.

'Actually, the theatre had not been looked after terribly well and looked
a bit shoddy and dirty. We had no control over the front of the house, of
course, but we had from the stage side and we decided to go to town on it.

'Jack told me how much we could spend on mounting the show and I
went over to London and Scotland hiring acts and costumes. We ended up
with a splendid and lavish production.'

Jimmy used the cast of the Bangor variety show but expanded the
company for the larger theatre. Tommy James now found himself at the
helm of a ten-piece orchestra and, instead of only two girl dancers, there
was a whole chorus line from Scotland called the Moxton Young Ladies.
Jimmy occasionally would have problems with these dancers, according to
Jean Lundy.

'Jimmy loved good outfits for the dancing troupes and he would spend
money on the most outrageous things, just so the audience would go,
"Ooh, look at that!"

'On one occasion, Jimmy rang up May Moxton and said, "I have two
complaints about your dancers, May. Firstly, I would rather the girls were

Leonard McNeill, one of The Young Voices

dressed in something that had a wee bit more *oomph*."

'So May replied, "Well, okay, what if I stick a cheeky wee bow on their bums?"

'Then Jimmy said, "That's fine. Secondly, the last girl of the line is too slow getting off the stage. As the music finishes, her face is off but her backside isn't."

'Then May said, "Jimmy, son, I can put a cheeky wee bow on her bum, but I can't screw the arse off her!"'

The show required 19 set changes, with Jimmy and Jack appearing in eight comedy sketches. No expense was spared and Jack was even able to order specially made drop cloths from England.

'We poured more and more money into the shows,' Jack said later, 'and I think we were the first people to bring male dancers and ballerinas to Belfast revue, as opposed to lines of kicking chorus girls which were then starting to go out of date. It was the biggest show, the most spectacular show, and the best dressed show that I could possibly put on.'

The first live show premiered on 17 November 1953, playing twice nightly for a seven-day trial run. During that week the box office took in more money than for any other show in the entire history of the Empire Theatre.

It was then that George Lodge, the Opera House's owner, made his approach.

Jimmy happily recalled: 'True to the promise he had given us before, Mr. Lodge offered us the Opera House for a week at Easter in 1954. At last my dream of appearing in my own show (there) was coming true.'

As the Opera House was a larger theatre than the Empire, the

Jimmy, Leonard McNeill and others at the 1958 Bangor Horse Show

performances had to be even more lavish than before. Jimmy 'wanted to put on a full-scale spectacular', and brought in many artists from London.

'But for one number,' he recalled, 'I wanted a boy soprano and auditioned hundreds of youngsters until I found one young lad with the most wonderful voice. His name was Leonard McNeill and he was a tremendous success. He was later to become a very good friend of mine and stayed with my company for many years.'

Leonard McNeill tells how he became involved in the show as a member of The Young Voices.

'Jimmy Young was looking for five choristers to do the Jimmy Brown song that goes, "All the chapel bells were ringing in the little valley town". He wanted a group of choristers at one side of the stage while this was all being enacted behind a piece of muslin like a ghost scene. Tommy James' son, Terry, was a choirboy in St George's church at the time and Tommy suggested holding auditions there. So Jimmy Young, Jack Hudson and Tommy James came along to choir practise one night and picked five of the choirboys, Terry and I being two of them.'

George Lodge insisted on Monday and Tuesday matinees, meaning more dress rehearsals on Sunday. This added to an already inflated budget. It was a big risk for James Young Productions as the show was costing in excess of £1,000 to stage. If it didn't succeed, Jimmy and Jack would be financially ruined. To alleviate some of the monetary stress on the partners, Lodge guaranteed them at least £1,000 from the box office taking, no matter if the show made a profit or a loss.

As it transpired, however, fears of failure proved unfounded. The Opera House shows were completely booked out and turned a profit in excess of £2,500. Years later, Jimmy would emotionally recollect his first performance there.

Jimmy and Jack onstage at the Opera House

'I will always remember the opening night of that show and waiting in the wings to go on stage. I always have nerves before a show but that night was far worse. After so much heartache and tears and so many years, I had achieved one thing I had really set my heart on. And as I walked down the steps onto the stage, the audience seemed to erupt, the applause was tremendous and you could feel the warmth coming up from them. This was one of the really big moments of my life. I have to admit, rather than wanting to be funny, I felt more like I wanted to cry. Jack and I had sunk pretty much every penny we had into staging that show. We put it into all the spectacle I had ever wanted to put into a revue and used the best scenery and acts we could afford.'

Unfortunately, future regular seasons at the Opera House were not possible as it was committed to touring companies and could only offer isolated weeks throughout the year. The Empire Theatre management, however, contracted the company to produce two eight-week seasons a year, one in the spring and another in the autumn, which they gladly accepted. The first of these new seasons started in February 1955.

In between these high profile engagements, Jimmy continued to bring his show on the road, into the town halls and small theatres of the north. It was during one of these tours, on 16 January 1954, that he received the news his father, who had been in failing health, had died. His mother had passed away 12 years earlier, causing Jimmy to forever regret that she had not lived to see him perform successfully at the venues he'd accompanied her to all those years before. On hearing about his father, Jimmy remembered 'trying to get the greasepaint over the tears, which were rolling down my face.'

That night, Jimmy had been booked to appear at an Orange Hall. He recalled: 'A man came in and told me, "There are at least 27 Catholics in the audience. We want you to walk out on to the stage and tell them to get out of the building, otherwise there will be no show." I told him that, if I were to do that, there would be no show for me either. They had come in to see me, not to hear a sermon on one religion or another. And I didn't do it and the audience remained.'

After a while, the popular success of the Empire theatre revues caught the attention of Hymie Zhal, who worked for one of the biggest promotional agencies in London. Travelling to Belfast to see the show for himself, he presented Jimmy and Jack with the opportunity to transfer to London.

'We had to have time to think this over,' Jimmy reflected, 'because taking the show to London would cost a lot of money. So I took Jack back to my house and made some supper and we talked into the early hours of the morning. Finally I said, "Jack, let's do it!" and he grinned and said, "Yes, let's." We would take the gamble.'

When word spread that the show was going to England, the nay-sayers re-emerged, stating that it was sure to fail because of the cast's Belfast accents. But Jimmy and his entourage proceeded, arriving at the Metropolitan Theatre in London with several tons of scenery and costumes.

On the first morning of rehearsals, they were a bit concerned when someone pieced together a torn-up letter they had found showing that the previous week's box office had been a sparse £420. With the £1,000 price tag for their show, things didn't look promising.

At that point, Jack said to Jimmy, 'Look, son, you'd better be good.'

A very small audience attended the opening night of the six-week run, confirming everybody's worst fears. But when the first of the newspaper reviews appeared, things slowly began to turn around. Positive word on the show caused the audiences to grow until, before long, people were being turned away from full houses. They made a reasonable profit in the end and, over the next few years, were able to successfully return many times to the same theatre.

With the promise of regular seasons at the Empire Theatre, Jimmy needed to find a source of new material for his shows. He found it in the shape of a young draughtsman called Sam Cree.

Sam, who was an aspiring writer, would regularly pen skits and parodies about his workplace at Knockmore in Lisburn. These would sometimes be recorded and played at Christmas parties, much to the amusement of his fellow workers. Spurred on by this low-key success, he submitted a script to Jimmy with a view to having it included in one of the summer revues.

According to Jack, the piece was 'the worst script I have ever read, from every point of view.'

Jimmy wrote to Sam, telling him that it was not suitable for a family audience, the dialogue was mindless and there wasn't one punch line in the

John Knipe, Jimmy's reliable songwriter, who provided him with the evergreen Slum Clearance

whole script. On top of this, since the sketch required a street of houses as the set, it was impossible to stage. However, Jimmy tempered his criticism by inviting Sam to see the type of material he was currently presenting in Bangor.

Sam took Jimmy's response to his script in his stride and was even heard boasting to friends that it was his first professional criticism.

He soon got a better grasp of what was required and began submitting material that Jimmy was more than happy to use. Within a short period of time, Sam's writing was never missing from the revues and he always had at least three sketches included in each show. Jimmy would brief Sam on the set-up for a sketch and Sam would be expected to quickly turn the idea into a workable script. Fortunately, he rose to the challenge and his writing skills rapidly developed under the guidance of his mentor.

Also entering the scene at this stage was John Knipe. A prominent figure in the Customs and Excise office in Belfast, Knipe dabbled in amateur dramatics on the side. He enjoyed a particularly successful sojourn as producer at the Bangor Amateur Dramatic Society, winning many awards for the company. He also displayed a knack for writing verses and comedy songs. Jimmy told later of his first encounter with Knipe.

'I first met John at that first season in Bangor. One evening, he had come backstage after the show. I had no idea that he was a writer but I explained to him that I needed something topical and bang up-to-date for the show, and he took out an envelope, sat down in the stalls, and jotted down one of the most amusing lyrics I have ever heard. We introduced it into the show the next week and it was a riot.'

An Empire Theatre programme sheet from the 50s

At first, Knipe would write new lyrics to the tunes of well-known songs, but progressed to putting words to original tunes composed by Jimmy. The composition process was novel as Jimmy had no musical aptitude whatsoever and couldn't play an instrument. But when he got a tune in his head, he would go to Tommy James and sing it. Tommy would write out the melody and play it to Knipe who, having got the general gist of the song idea from Jimmy, would then go off and complete it.

Knipe had his own unusual method of doing things, claiming that he could only write while travelling on the top of a bus. He would climb the stairs to the upper level of a Corporation bus and stay there until the song was complete.

It was while travelling by bus from Belfast's City Hall to Glengormley, via the Antrim Road, that Knipe penned what was to be the first of Jimmy's serious monologues. *Slum Clearance* was a comment on the effect of relocation on the people in the little back streets of Belfast. In the 1950s, Belfast City Council was tearing down many houses because of the low

The beginning of the end: The Empire Theatre before it was sold off

standard of living for their occupants. Many did not have inside toilets or hot running water. Jimmy had known the people of these communities in his younger days and appreciated their distress at being uprooted from the only homes they'd ever had.

From its opening where an old man laments, 'They have given me my notice, I must pack my bags and go,' the piece was to become a staple of Jimmy's act over the next 18 years. His emotional rendering of *Slum Clearance* never failed to move those who heard it.

With the revue shows at the Empire during the spring and autumn, the summer season in Bangor, the London shows and his radio series, Jimmy now had his diary fully booked. But that was to change when the Empire's owners decided to sell the lease on the venue. Initially, Jimmy expressed an interest.

'We decided we could not afford to let the Empire go because it had become our home in Belfast, so we approached the directors to see if we could buy it.'

The directors said that they were very interested in leasing the theatre to Jimmy. It would, however, have to be for a minimum of ten years at £5,000 a year. Additionally, money would be needed to upgrade the venue.

Jimmy's friend, J Ritchie McKee, warned him to be very careful and, at his own expense, sent in surveyors to check the building's structure. When McKee met the theatre's directors in Dublin, he realised that something was up. It transpired that a deal had already been done and the Empire's days were numbered. Eventually, the site would become a Littlewoods department store.

Jimmy was very sad to see the Empire go. Being the first theatre he had gone to all those years ago with his beloved mother, it had earned a special place in his affections. However, McKee, who was chairman of the Group, asked Jimmy and Jack, 'Why don't you both come into the Group and put on a play there?'

In common with other theatres at this time, the Group had fallen on hard times, due mainly to the onslaught of television. Where people had previously attended the theatre in the evenings, television now dictated that they could be entertained in the comfort of their own living rooms.

Other factors accentuated the Group's plight, however. For one, the mighty talent that had founded and built the theatre, making it possibly the most important showcase for new and challenging drama in Ireland, was being lured elsewhere. Audiences had flocked to see young bucks like Stephen Boyd, Colin Blakely and Patrick Magee on the Bedford Street

The long arm of the law. James Ellis in Z Cars: *as Artistic Director of the Group Theatre, however, he fell foul of the Board of Directors with his intentions of staging* Over The Bridge

Sam Thompson, whose controversial Over The Bridge *inadvertently paved the way for Jimmy's return to the Group Theatre*

stage. But when they joined the old guard of Tomelty, McAlinney, Harold Goldblatt, and Elizabeth Begley in accepting lucrative film and television work, as well as better paid stage appearances in London and New York, their absence only marked the scarcity of real talent emerging to take their places. Additionally, actors' wages were rising and the theatre could no longer pay its way. This factor was picked up on by Jack Hudson.

'They are paying out far more in wages every week than they could have possibly taken in box office receipts even if they had capacity houses,' he observed.

Indeed, on many occasions, the actors on stage outnumbered the people in the audience, as Jean Lundy recalls.

'One time, with this play, they cancelled the matinee because there were only three people in the audience and, apparently, it was an equity rule that, if the cast outnumbers the audience, the cast was entitled to strike.'

The Group's problems were compounded by the crisis over Sam Thompson's play, *Over the Bridge*.

Born in 1916 in Belfast, Thompson had been an apprentice painter in Harland & Wolff shipyard. As a committed trade union and labour activist, later standing for election with the Northern Ireland Labour Party, he had been dismissed from his job at Belfast Corporation when he became the union shop steward. Turning to writing and acting, he joined the Group and became determined to write a play that would expose the bigotry and discrimination going unchecked at the shipyard. The result was *Over the Bridge*.

Aware of the volatile subject matter, Thompson had informed James Ellis, the Group's Artistic Director at this point, 'I've written a play but you won't touch it.'

Ellis was immediately convinced that this was a play that had to be staged and received the go-ahead from the reading committee at the theatre. However, the Board of Directors was not so enthusiastic. Appalled that such a production was being planned for their theatre, they issued a statement through J Ritchie McKee which said that they were 'determined not to mount any play which would offend or affront any religious beliefs or sensitivities of the man in the street of any denomination or class in the community and which would give rise to sectarian or political controversy of an extreme nature.'

The play was withdrawn and, disgusted at the blatant censorship of the board, key Group players, including Ellis, resigned their posts. Ellis, who was to become one of the north's most popular and enduring actors through his roles in *Z Cars* and the *Billy* plays on television, did manage to successfully stage a production of *Over the Bridge*. Ironically, this was at the Empire Theatre.

Boosted by this success, the Group rebels presented other plays at the Empire but the writing was already on the wall for the venue.

Jimmy, however, recalled that someone did profit from the Empire's problems.

'I remember, at this time, a very astute gentleman from the south of Ireland set up a caravan outside the Empire and started a "Save the Theatre" fund. Lots of theatre lovers handed over five bobs, ten bobs and pound notes but he later disappeared into the blue and was never heard of again.'

Back at the Group, J Ritchie McKee, looking for a safe pair of hands to take the helm at Bedford Street, turned to Jimmy. McKee believed that non-controversial comic plays were surefire money earners among local audiences. This belief was confirmed by the popularity of a touring production of Gerald McNamara's *No Surrender* with J G Devlin, which had managed to stave off financial disaster for a while. Knowing that this genre was Jimmy's forte, McKee was determined to woo him on to the Group's stage in a bid to get bums on seats at the ailing theatre.

With the loss of the Empire, Jimmy was also desperate to find a permanent base in Belfast. It seemed to him that the Group, where he had started his stage career, could work out to be the place he needed.

5

James Young returned to the stage of the Group Theatre on 8 March 1960 in a play written by Glenn Melvyn, an actor he'd replaced when he had first gone to Manchester to perform in repertory there.

The Love Match had been a minor hit while touring its home turf in the north of England and was even filmed in 1955 with its original star, Arthur Askey. John Keyes, who had acted alongside Askey in the touring production, explains how he brought the play to Jimmy's attention.

Group Theatre programme

'It struck me as being a good vehicle for James Young whom I had known and admired for years… I sent (the play) to Jimmy who engaged a young man to rewrite it for him translating the plot to Belfast and ensuring the usual quota of Orange and Green humour. The writer's name was Sam Cree.'

Among the alterations devised by Sam was changing the original's central character, a keen Bolton Wanderers supporter, into Alex Galbraith, a Linfield fanatic. The plot of the play involves Alex's son getting picked for Glentoran Football Club, much to his father's disgust. After many comic developments, it all comes to a happy ending with Alex, played by Jimmy, cheering as his son scores the winning goal in the Cup.

In keeping with the theme of the play, Jimmy invited players from the real Linfield and Glentoran football teams to the opening night. These included the Linfield captain Jackie Milburn and his Glentoran equal, Billy Neill. J Ritchie McKee's belief that Jimmy in a local comedy would be lucrative for the theatre was proven correct and the play was sold out at every performance.

The Love Match partnered Jimmy with an actress who would feature heavily in his future stage and television career. She would become one of his closest friends and, to this day, is firmly associated with Jimmy and his shows. Her name was Jean Lundy. Jimmy always spoke of Jean in glowing terms.

'When the part of Emily Beattie came up in *The Love Match*, I knew there was only one person to play her and that was Jean. But she had had a very unhappy experience with the previous company at the Group and, although she loves acting, she was very dubious about taking on this part.'

The departure of James Ellis and the old Group players had left a sour taste in Jean's mouth and she felt that she was unable to return to the place where there had been so much acrimony and recrimination. As she now recalls:

'Jimmy phoned me and asked me to come down and take a part in his new play and I said, "No, I wasn't going back to the Group because I was sick of all the fighting and quarrelling."

'Now Jimmy was a very good friend of Elizabeth Begley, another Group actress, and she said to him, "Don't ask her directly to take part in the play. Just ask her to come down and help out because you're short of someone. Once she gets involved she'll be hooked."

'So Jimmy phoned me up and said that the actress playing the part of Emily Beattie had taken ill and could I come down and read the part to help with the rehearsals?

'And I said, "Jimmy, are you perfectly clear that I will not be taking a part in your play?" These were, of course, famous last words for I came down and ended up playing the same role for the next 12 years.'

Much like Jimmy, Jean had started her acting career with the Group in the early 1940s, one of her first performances being in St John Irvine's play, *Boyd's Shop*. Today, Jean looks back happily on those days.

'I was only 16 in 1940 when *Boyd's Shop* opened at the Group. My family came from Carrickfergus but we had friends who lived off York Road and it was agreed that I could stay at their house to save me travelling back and forward. Before this was arranged, my mother thought it was terrible that I was travelling all the way to Belfast. So Bob Dempster, a great actor, who played Andrew Boyd in the play and also came from Carrick, told my mother that he would escort me home on the last train every night at ten o'clock.

'What my mother didn't know, however, was that after the show, before we got on the train to go home, we would call into the Buffs club for a drink. That's where I first learned to drink gin.'

The cast list for The Love Match, *Jimmy's first production on his return to the Group in 1960*

"THE LOVE MATCH"

SAM CREE'S Ulster Adaptation of the Comedy by GLENN MELVYN

Characters in order of appearance

SADIE GALBRAITH	Melda Davey
MYRA GALBRAITH (her daughter)	May Diver
ARTHUR FORD	Jack Hudson
DAVIE GALBRAITH (Sadie's son)	Terry Cromey
WILLIE BEATTIE	John F. Tyrone
EMILY BEATTIE (his wife)	Jean Lundy
ALEC GALBRAITH (Sadie's husband)	James Young
DENNIS HALL	Hugh Swandell
CONSTABLE	Maurice O'Callaghan

The Play Produced by JAMES YOUNG and JONATHAN GOODMAN

In *Boyd's Shop*, Jean played one of the gossiping local girls who spent all of their time in the grocer's shop talking about their neighbours. Jimmy had witnessed her performance in this play and remarked that, even in this small role, she was a natural scene-stealer with a beautiful sense of comedy.

Her part in *The Love Match* was in a similar vein. She played Jimmy's next door neighbour, Emily Beattie, a lady who was always short of money and had the habit of popping in to borrow a cup of sugar or a 'wee drop of milk' for her husband Willie's tea. Another Young regular, John F Tyrone, took on the part of Willie. Jean's name would become synonymous with Emily Beattie and she was to play the part on stage and television for many years to come.

The Love Match was only able to run for ten weeks as Jimmy was still tied to his Bangor summer season for that year. The Group was also committed to staging two more plays. But, before the end of the run, J Ritchie McKee and the Board of Directors invited Jimmy and Jack to join the theatre on a permanent basis.

Accepting this offer would be a major decision on their part for, although they had lost the Empire shows, they were still doing well financially from the summer season, the provincial tours and various BBC shows. Jimmy and Jack decided to give it a shot and signed up exclusively to the running of the Group. The only proviso they insisted on was that they be given a completely free hand in its administration.

After years of financial difficulties, the theatre was in a bad state of repair and looked dirty and tatty. Jimmy set about improving things immediately, guided by his notion of what going to the theatre should be like.

'Our policy has always been that, for the audience, the show begins not when the curtain goes up but the moment they arrive in the theatre. It needs carpets and comfortable seats and pleasant surroundings. A visit to the theatre should be an occasion. But, at that time, the Group was really just a minor part of the Ulster Hall and very bare at that. As soon as we moved in, we began to renovate it, repairing, altering and adding whatever we thought necessary. And, most of all, we wanted to make it economical. We didn't want to have to rely on Arts Council money.'

James Young and Jack Hudson became Managing Directors of the Group in the autumn of 1960. It was to be their theatrical home for the next 11 years.

Now that they had their own theatre, the next step was to find a suitable play and start to generate some more money.

Sam Cree came up with the goods in the shape of *Wedding Fever*, a new play based around the characters featured in *The Love Match*. Jimmy once again played the central character of Alex Galbraith with Melda Davey as his wife Sadie. Jean Lundy and John F Tyrone reprised the roles of Emily and Willie Beattie, while Jack Hudson and Della Beck played the Hingleheifers, visiting relations from America. The cast was completed with Terence Cromey as the son, Davy Galbraith, and May Diver as Myra, the daughter around whose wedding the action revolved.

Opening on 28 September 1960, many of the political figures of the day attended. The Prime Minister of Northern Ireland and his wife, Lord and Lady Brookeborough, Belfast Lord Mayor, Sir Robin Kinahan, and many of the aldermen and councillors of the city were in attendance at the premiere, decked out in appropriate finery. As a generous gesture, Jimmy donated the entire proceeds of the evening to the rebuilding fund for the new Arts Theatre, which was soon to open in Botanic Avenue. Although he was, in effect, funding his own competition, Jimmy was more than happy to assist in providing more entertainment for the people of Belfast.

Wedding Fever is a show filled with laughter until the very last scene when Alex and his daughter are left alone in the house, waiting for the bridal car. To calm his daughter's nerves, he reminisces about how he nursed her as a baby, their holidays together and other memories of her childhood. Jimmy's delivery of this speech was touching and, as the curtain came down with May and him walking arm in arm upstage to the door, there were few dry eyes in the audience.

This scene was particularly poignant for May Diver as her own father had become terminally ill during the run of the play. Jimmy offered to get a stand-in but May found a certain comfort in the role and bravely carried on until the end of the run.

Wedding Fever proved to be another success and allowed Jimmy to pay off the outstanding debt owed by the theatre to the Arts Council.

Jimmy relocated his Bangor summer shows to Belfast, and the Group revues were born

---

JAMES YOUNG - in - *the group revue*

Derek Marsden, introduces the Show and the Company with Jack Hudson and James Young.

The Kerry Dancers: Tom Conwell and Leonard McNeill.

City Tour: No. I, The Courtroom; No. 2, as others see us.

Tom Conwell.

Press Correspondents: Melda Davey, Jean Lundy Jack Hudson and James Young.

Music Hath Charms.

Man Wanted: Jean Lundy, Jack Hudson, May Diver and James Young.

The Young Voices.

Granny's Photo Album.

INTERVAL

Harps of Ireland: Tom Conwell and Leonard McNeill introduce.

Mary McEvoy.

Slum Clearance.

Derek Marsden.

Face to Face: Jack Hudson as John Freeman meets . . . . .

The Angelus: Tom Conwell, featuring The Young Voices.

The Wallflowers: Melda Davey, Jack Hudson and James Young.

The Recordites.

Travel Talk: Jack Hudson and James Young.

The Company say Good Night.

★ ★ Tea and Soft Drinks may be obtained in the Foyer during the Interval ★ ★

'Before *The Love Match* the Group had been heavily in debt but thi
play got them out of it. But later, when we came back after the summe
break, we found that an English director had not only lost all the mone
we had made but had also had to borrow £1,000 … in order to pay th
salaries. So we came back to the Group and one of the most satisfyin
things that happened to me was that, with the next play we put on, w
were able to pay back the whole of the £1,000 that had been borrowe
from the Arts Council.'

Having sacrificed his Bangor variety revue to concentrate on the Group
Jimmy decided to transfer the format of his old summer season shows t
the Belfast theatre. All the regular faces (Jean Lundy, Melda Davey, Jac
Hudson et al) performed the traditional blend of sketches and music
Interludes were provided by tenor Tom Conwell, an eight-piece boy's choi
called The Young Voices, harpist Mary McEvoy, a mime troupe called Th
Recordites, and old friend, Leonard McNeill, who did a spot of Iris
dancing. Derek Marsden, later to become a popular Downtown Radi
presenter and host of *Date with Derek*, provided accompaniment for th
acts on the piano and theatre organ.

It was around this time that the creative partnership with Sam Cre
came to an end. Seeking a career out from under Jimmy's shadow and

Jimmy Logan in a Sam Cree comedy, after Cree ended his partnership with Jimmy

John McDonnell. His play, All The King's Horses, *began a partnership with Jimmy that would last over ten years*

wishing to write plays without any interference from the star of the show, Sam formed a partnership with the Scottish actor and music hall performer, Jimmy Logan. Logan had a long association with Northern Ireland and had appeared many times at the Empire. Jimmy Logan and James Young had actually become quite good friends over the years and Logan had stayed at Jimmy's Belfast home many times while touring.

After writing for Logan for a few years, Sam eventually returned to Belfast and began a long association as the virtual writer in residence at the Arts Theatre.

Sam's departure left Jimmy searching for a replacement. Luckily, he'd heard about a new play that had run for two weeks at Dublin's Abbey Theatre. *All the King's Horses* was written by Dublin journalist, John McDonnell, and had been well received. Reading a review of the play, Jimmy was taken by its central premise and contacted the author. As usual, however, Jimmy thought that the piece would need reworking for a northern audience.

'As it had already been on at the Abbey, John ... would have been perfectly entitled to fly off the handle at the suggestion that anything should be changed but, instead, he listened patiently while I made a lot of suggestions about changes, including writing in an additional character. It was that of an English visitor, someone who knew nothing of Irish politics, and this part was eventually played, superbly, by Jack Hudson.'

Jimmy's meeting with John McDonnell was the start of long and lasting friendship. Jimmy was to compliment John with the following words.

'John has no arty airs about him and, being a journalist, set about the changes I suggested in a most realistic fashion. He shoved a piece of paper into his typewriter and started writing. Inside a week he had a completely rewritten version of *All the King's Horses* on my desk. And he told me, "Do with the play what you think fit. You know your audience better than I do." After the first night, he came up to me and said he was absolutely delighted with it.'

Indeed, as John Keyes points out, 'Jimmy didn't need a writer. Just someone to provide him with a story board which he would fill in at rehearsals.'

In the play, a wealthy old southern woman called Kate Houlihan is dying and her last request is to see her two nephews. One is Michael Maloney, a staunch republican from the south, while the other is William McStay, a true blue loyalist from Belfast, played by Jimmy. They meet at their aunt's deathbed and, not unexpectedly, they fail to get along. The old woman dies and, in her will, leaves her house and all her money to the nephews. However, the will stipulates that her bequest is to be divided equally between them on one condition – they must live together in her

Jimmy answering fan mail

house for one month in peace and harmony. If they do not, all of the inheritance goes to the church.

In the course of the play, the nephews have to work out how to live together. They partition the house with a chalk line down the centre of the wall, across the floor and dividing the dining room table. On one side of the line hangs a Union Jack and a portrait of Queen Elizabeth II while, on the other, an Irish tricolour and a photograph of Irish President, Eamon De Valera, are prominent.

The play is a typical James Young farce with comedy arising out of situations such as how the radio can be operated when the set is on one side of the divide with the plug hole on the other. But, for local audiences it proved a tonic and the Group had another hit on its hands. As a result the only author's name associated with the Group for the next ten years was John McDonnell who, in collaboration with Jimmy, developed a production line approach to writing, churning out play after play to sate the public appetite for broad comedy.

For the summer season, Jimmy would try and think of something with a holiday theme. If it was the autumn and winter season, he would devise another Galbraith family farce or something with an Orange and Green theme. When Jimmy had a rough idea of what he wanted to do there would follow several long telephone calls to Dublin where McDonnell would make a start on the script. Jimmy outlined the basic story and told McDonnell which actors should have the major roles and McDonnell would write parts that suited them.

One of Jimmy's friends and associates around this time, actor Frank Crummey, recalls how the writing of the plays developed.

'John McDonnell would send up the first act on a Sunday morning and, by Sunday afternoon, it was a completely different script. Jimmy would go, "Right, put that bit in; right, take that bit out." He changed the whole thing, trying to make it as funny as possible. This would go on through all the various drafts with changes being made continually. I remember times when we were only getting the final script on the Saturday and the play was starting on Monday.'

McDonnell and his wife Patti routinely came to the first night of a new play and it became a standing joke that he would always exclaim, 'A lovely play, Jimmy. I'm so glad you used my title!'

As with many of Jimmy's plays, the local press were less than kind about *All the King's Horses*, regarding such fare as lowbrow, even though the shows played to packed houses every evening.

As Ivan Martin says, 'The critics hated it. It wasn't art and, because it wasn't art, it wasn't acceptable. You frowned on it.'

Jimmy always had an answer for these critics.

'It's inevitable that we've been criticised for this commercial policy of ours. There are dozens of people that think we should be the "vanguard of the Ulster theatrical renaissance". If this means putting on Celtic twilight stuff about the early childhood of Brian Boru to an audience of six, then

Jimmy in a signed portrait shot, circa 1965

I'm not interested. I am in this business for money, though even if I wasn't making a living at it, my hobby would still be the theatre.'

While he accepted criticism aimed at himself, he would not stand for any directed at his close friends. On one occasion, when a newspaper review slated Jack Hudson's sets as being over elaborate, Jimmy sent the offending critic a 'drop dead' card and a tin of cat food. He was delighted to hear she was deeply affronted.

Jimmy, who had started his career with the Youth Hostel Association Drama Group, never lost his interest in the amateur theatre. He was unfailing in his encouragement of promising young actors and actresses from local dramatic

*The James Young
Gold Award*

societies and gave many youngsters their start in the business. One such person was John O'Hara, who would later become one of Ulster Television's top announcers.

*Jimmy and Jack on
the stairs of their
Roddens Park home*

'I was just one of many he helped,' said O'Hara. 'And, in later years when things were not going so well, he gave encouragement and examples of how times hadn't always been good for him either. He was a master of his art and he knew it. He was very much a 'somebody'. I remember when I was working at the Group Theatre in the early 60s, he was driving me home after a performance when suddenly, without warning, a woman driver appeared from nowhere and almost rammed him. He slammed on the brakes, jumped from the car, rushed up to the visibly shaken woman and shouted "Are you mad, madam? I'm James Young."

Jimmy's relationship with Jack at this time had become less personal and more business oriented. He had moved with Jack to 24 Roddens Park, on the edge of the Braniel estate, in the 1950s but eventually, Jack moved into a flat of his own. The two remained best of friends however, and Jack supported Jimmy in establishing an award for the best amateur actor at the annual Northern Ireland Drama Festival, an accolade Jimmy had won all those years before.

The trophy was a medallion on a chain, worked in gold and depicting the comedy and tragedy masks. It was known as the *Group Theatre Gold Award* but is presented to budding young thespians today as the *James Young Gold Award*.

Jack was to refer to the trophy as 'one of many small things which will help to perpetuate Jimmy's memory through the years in the field that was his first and last love – the theatre.'

Riding the crest of a wave at this point in his career, fate was to step in again and provide another opening, albeit through the death of a close friend.

'In the middle of the night, the telephone by the side of my bed rang and I answered it, very sleepily. It was one of J Ritchie McKee's children, and he said, "I've very bad news for you. Daddy has died."'

McKee had died while on holiday with his wife in the United States. His death came as a tremendous shock to Jimmy, Jack and the company at the Group. It also meant that his seat on the Group's Board of Directors was now vacant. When Jimmy proposed that McKee's widow, Ada, should take the vacant seat as a tribute to her husband's memory, he was overruled.

'The unanimous decision of the Board was that I should become chairman in Ritchie's place.'

6

The cast of Friends and Neighbours. *Frank Crummey is to the left of Jack Hudson in the back row*

As the new chairman of the Group Theatre's Board of Directors, Jimmy could take pride in that he reigned over hit play after hit play at the Bedford Street venue during the 1960s. That he was also the creator, producer and star of these plays was an added bonus. *Friends and Neighbours, Love Locked Out, An Apple a Day, Wish You Were Here, Silver*

The cast of Friends and Neighbours. *Frank Crummey is to the left of Jack Hudson in the back row*

A typical example of the 'wee Belfast men' played by Jimmy: Big Aggie's Man

Wedding and *Holiday Spirit* provided the theatre with a roll call of plays which were hugely popular with the public.

Friends and Neighbours, adapted by John McDonnell from an original play by Austin Steele, had a record run of ten months. The box office receipts totalled £20,500 – an incredible amount for the period. The Group held almost 300 people and was packed every night. Parties as diverse as Orange lodges and women's guilds would block book and the theatre would be sold out three or four months in advance.

Jimmy attributed the production's popularity to the fact that all sections of the community had been represented in it. He also believed that people could associate with the typical Belfast man he portrayed onstage.

'You know, the wee Belfast men I play in all the Group Theatre productions… are representative of the vast majority of wee Belfast men you see packing the streets. There's nothing airy-fairy about them. They're frank to the point of bluntness. They speak out forcefully and don't pull punches. They may have prejudices but they are sincerely held.

'When it's the wife's birthday, he'll not rush up behind her and nibble her ear while murmuring sweet nothings before whipping out big bunches of flowers. No, he'll fling a brown paper parcel on the sideboard and say, "There's a wee something I've got you. I hope it's your right size," before disappearing upstairs until he stops blushing.

'When a boyo stops me in street and says, "We were at the show last week. It was pretty good. The wife nearly *boked*, she was laughing so much," that pleases me a hundred times more than some gusher running up screaming, "Darling, you were wonderful!" That never happens here but I had a bellyful of it in England.'

The plot of *Love Locked Out* – the next Young and McDonnell collaboration, based on a play by David Kirk – revolves around three factory workers who go on strike when a fellow-worker is denied an annual allowance for the purchase of bicycle clips. Their wives then gang up and go on strike themselves in an effort to get their errant husbands to 'catch themselves on'. The play contained the origins of one of the most memorable characters to feature in Jimmy's later BBC television series: the trade union man, whose sole aim in life seemed to be to prevent his union members from doing any actual work. A self-proclaimed 'strike starter', he would call for the downing of tools at the most meagre of excuses, such as management's refusal to provide saucers for mugs, before uttering his catch phrase: 'It's not the first time, and it won't be the last.'

On many occasions, Jimmy delighted in trying to distract his fellow cast members by whispering something comical in their ears during a play. Frank Crummey, a young actor who had recently joined the Group, was at the receiving end of this during one performance of *Love Locked Out*.

'There was one night, I'll never forget it. (Jimmy) was dressed up as a big blonde with a cream coat on. In the scene, John McDade was playing a hen-pecked husband and Jimmy, as the blonde, was playing up to him. McDade's wife appears and sees the big blonde all over her husband and wheels him out. My part was to run down the stairs and deliver a line but as I came down, I could see that twinkle in Jimmy's eye and the next thing he leaned over and whispered in my ear, "McDade has a hard on."

'And I just exploded and burst out laughing, and then the audience started to laugh. The more I laughed, the more they laughed. Every time I went to say the line he would go, "He has, look, look, it's like a wee wriggly worm!" And he kept that going for five or six minutes until the moment he knew the joke was milked. Then a look came over his face because he knew he'd got the laugh out of it. Then it was deep breaths and on with the play.'

Jimmy as Sadie, a lady fond of the odd tipple or two

Love Locked Out ran for five months until October 1963.

James Young was now one of the most famous people in Northern Ireland and, although he loved the attention, he also acknowledged its downside at the time.

'There are a few drawbacks to being well known. For a start some people think that, just because you are in the theatre business, you should operate something like a free advice service for parents of talented children. I'm not talking about young people who come for auditions. I'm always delighted to meet potential actors.

'The people I mean are the folk who turn up in the Group before the show and ask my opinion about little Sadie's tap dancing or little Johnny's golden voice, and can I get them on television or something.

One of Jimmy's many female characters

Unfortunately, I can rarely do anything useful for them.

'I was continually plagued with calls from all sorts of people when my number was on the open list. Many of them were friendly and well intentioned but, even then, I didn't much fancy being told at midnight how much so and so enjoyed the show.

'Others were not so well intentioned. One gentleman used to ring about three in the morning and keep ringing until I answered. When I did, he would breathe heavily and whisper that he was "coming to get me with a hatchet". I was never over amused.'

Frank Crummey states that all was not sweetness and light with Jimmy.

'In one play, I was this daft character and I had a line where I said something to a Catholic woman about the Pope. Jimmy then said, "What

Jimmy and Jack discussing the takings for the Galbraith Family comedy, Silver Wedding

the hell did you come out with that for? Don't you know she's a Catholic?"

'My reply was, "Well, I knew she was a Catholic but I didn't know the Pope was!"

'This got a belter of a laugh the first night, a belter of a laugh the second night. But on the third night, just as I said the punch line, Jimmy turned his back on me and walked to the other side of the stage, killing the joke dead and, as a result, no laugh.'

Between 1964 and 1965 Jimmy and the Group players were busy with productions of *Silver Wedding*, considered by many to be John McDonnell's best play since *All the King's Horses*, and *Holiday Spirit*. The former, which ran for seven months, dealt with the build up to the Galbraiths' wedding anniversary while the latter had a supernatural theme.

In *Holiday Spirit*, set in a boarding house in Portrush, Jimmy played two parts: one was a ghost dressed in drag and the other a camp scoutmaster called Harold Swann. Swann, who was a bit of a 'mammy's boy', was another in the long list of effeminate men portrayed by Jimmy, dating back to Derek the window cleaner. The character would later evolve into Big Derek on his television show.

In an interview published around this time, Jimmy explained why he was attracted to playing such camp figures.

'There's something pathetic about nearly every comic character, from Chaplin's Little Man all the way through to current television comedy buffoons. Take the example of the Harold Swann character ... He's an effeminate little scoutmaster who is completely dominated by his mother.

Rowel Friers poster for Sticks and Stones

He is preoccupied by little fussy things like his knitting and his cat and his budgie. If he doesn't get his breakfast dead on eight o'clock his day isn't right. In many ways these eccentricities make him funny. But remove him from the context of a comedy play and he's a pathetically sad little person indeed. This type of character is perfect for Belfast comedy as they can evoke tears and laughter from the audience.'

Next up, in the autumn of 1965, was John McDonnell's *Sticks and Stones*. Jimmy played the owner of a small corner grocery shop who has received a notice from the local council. They have decided to knock his shop down in order for the road to be widened. Jimmy's character is resigned to this fact until one of his

Publicity still of the young Philip Mulholland

customers informs him that the 'dirty, filthy Catholic shop' on the other corner is being allowed to stay.

This, of course, has the local Protestant community up in arms and they start to petition local government at Stormont. Events escalate until the Queens Consul from London is sent along and sets up a meeting to explain the situation to the people. Jimmy organises a protest march to the hall, complete with a flute band, and a fight starts. The entire company took part in the march, tramping down the aisles of the theatre to the music of recorded bands.

Philip Mulholland played one of the arresting police officers in the play.

'My role had, in fact, quite an interesting genesis. Jimmy, always ready to draw inspiration from those he met, based it, in part, on Leonard McNeill. He had quit the theatre when Jimmy stopped producing his variety shows, and had fulfilled his ambition to join the Royal Ulster Constabulary. Jimmy even named the character Constable Leonard Crawford, Crawford being the name of his pet poodle which was so called because of Jimmy's fondness for dining at the Crawfordsburn Inn when he went to visit Jean.'

As the marching scene required Jimmy to wear a sash, he asked a local Orange lodge to lend him one but was given a polite refusal. He then decided to get one made and went to the shop in Belfast that specialised in them. However, sashes could only be made for authentic lodges so they too refused. In desperation, Jimmy went to a company who manufactured sashes for the Catholic Ancient Order of Hibernians. They were happy to oblige, although the finished article was lined with green silk. They put a fictitious lodge number on it, which was several thousand more than the highest possible number of lodges in existence, but there were still complaints from people who thought Jimmy was being disrespectful.

During one performance, Philip Mulholland and Frank Crummey had to take their roles as RUC officers a little too far, as Philip remembers.

'As the cast relaxed in the dressing rooms during the intermission, one of the pageboys came running up the stairs in an obviously distressed state to report that loud screams could be heard from the ladies toilets. Jimmy, who had heard the commotion from his own dressing room, quickly organised a posse of some of the male cast members, including Frank Crummey and myself, to investigate.

'We found a small crowd of patrons gathered outside the ladies toilets comforting a very upset young woman. She reported to Jimmy that, on entering one of the cubicles, she had suddenly been confronted by two large males climbing through the window above her head, and she believed that they were still inside.

'Jimmy quickly sent someone to call the police and tried to figure out what to do next. Frank told Jimmy that he and I, dressed in our police uniforms, would rush in with batons drawn shouting, "Police, don't move!"

'Jimmy slowly opened the door a fraction, reached in and turned off the light, and Frank and I led the charge into the toilets only to find one small and very frightened youth who, being unable to reach the window again, was cowering miserably in the cubicle.

'Shortly after, the real police arrived and I can remember the bemused look on their faces when they were confronted by these two somewhat young looking peelers wearing orange makeup, eye shadow and rouge.'

It transpired that the young intruder and a friend had been trying to gain access to the Ulster Hall to watch the boxing there. Jimmy took pity on the two, pressing no charges, and they were released with a caution from the police. The lady they had startled was rewarded with a box of chocolates from Jimmy for her minor ordeal.

The cast of Sticks and Stones

As theatregoers were arriving on opening night to see *Sticks and Stones*, they were greeted by a Shankill Road flute band playing outside. Jimmy had hired the band as a stunt, thinking it would get him some good publicity. However, there was amateur boxing on the Ulster Hall's bill that night with a large Catholic crowd in attendance. Jimmy had given the band strict orders not to play any 'party tunes' but this had been wishful thinking on his part. On the way out, the theatre's patrons were treated to a re-enactment of the show with rival factions fighting it out in Bedford Street. Jimmy got his publicity but, perhaps, not the kind he was aiming for.

Another addition to Jimmy's regular players at this point was Ivan Martin. Now a popular local broadcaster, Ivan joined the cast of *Sticks and Stones* as a fresh-faced 13 year-old Methody schoolboy. His mother had won tickets to one of Jimmy's previous plays and had written to thank him, mentioning by the way that her son had a great love of the theatre. Jimmy responded to the letter, complimenting Mrs Martin on her thoughtfulness, and asked her to send young Ivan down for an audition if he was interested.

Ivan went for the audition, impressed Jimmy, and appeared in several Group productions until being forced back to school to concentrate on his exams. He later summed up what it was like to work alongside Jimmy.

'He was great fun to be with. He had travelled the world and had loads of stories to tell. He was a real stickler for detail and spent endless time rehearsing lines. But he was larger than life and was very good to the people who worked with him.'

Jack Hudson, Jimmy and Jean Lundy in a scene from Lucky Break

For the summer season of 1966, Jimmy devised a play that harked back to his old variety and revue shows. Entitled *Lucky Break*, it had a very large, mostly amateur, cast, including a singer and two Spanish dancers. Jimmy played Lucky, a punch-drunk ex-boxer with slurred speech, flattened nose and cauliflower ears. The character was apparently based on the well-known Belfast boxer, Rinty Monaghan.

'The play opened to great acclaim,' says Philip Mulholland, 'and seemed set for a long run but, as summer approached, when the play would usually be rested for four weeks, there were signs that all was not well and that Jimmy was growing increasingly fed up with the whole production.'

From the start, Jimmy had been plagued by some of the less professional members of the cast. One individual in particular consistently showed up drunk for work, drank from a hip flask between scenes, and was causing all sorts of problems for the rest of the company. This person had only been hired as a favour to his wealthy and influential family and Jimmy was very reluctant to sack him.

Meanwhile, at great expense and amid massive publicity, Jimmy and Jack had launched a restaurant and coffee lounge called *The Intermission* in the old printer's shop next to the theatre. Named after Jack's private yacht, the whole enterprise had started running at a loss almost from the day it opened.

To compound these problems, the theatre box office was suffering due to the glorious summer weather. It was one of the very few times that empty seats could be found in the front rows of the Group Theatre.

To cut costs, Jimmy and Jack decided not to reopen *Lucky Break* after the summer recess and to sacrifice their holidays in order to get a new show written and rehearsed. It was decided to have a much smaller cast for the next production and to forego using amateur actors who had made up the numbers in the *Lucky Break* cast.

'Another thing that happened was the road accident Jimmy and I were involved in,' Philip recalls. 'An articulated lorry's brakes had failed and it hit Jimmy's car, completely destroying it from just behind the front seats, leaving us both extremely shaken but unhurt. So now Jimmy had the added burden, at least until the matter of insurance could be settled, of financing a new car.'

This left Jimmy with no means of transport and he started to travel to the theatre by bus, much to the amusement of the other passengers. This continued for a few weeks and everyone at the theatre, including Jack, wondered why Jimmy had not replaced his car. What they didn't know was that he had already bought himself a brand new Volvo. The problem was that he was afraid that Jack would be angry at such extravagance and had

Jimmy bringing Christmas cheer to a crewman aboard HMS Maidstone

decided to leave it at home when he went to the theatre. He continued to travel to and from work by bus and taxi until he felt ready to tell Jack about his new purchase.

One night, as Jimmy travelled home, he struck up his usual conversation with the taxi driver. The story goes that the driver on this occasion was none other than Francie McPeake, of the McPeake family of musicians, composers of *Wild Mountain Thyme* and many other folk music standards. Arriving at Jimmy's house, Francie refused to take his fare but, after some coaxing, he accepted an invitation to come in for a night-cap.

Relaxing in Jimmy's lounge, Francie described how it was very hard to make a living in Belfast from music alone, hence the driving job. Jimmy joked that he might have to start driving a taxi after work as well, telling Francie some of his own ongoing problems.

It was then that Francie commented that people only really went to the Group Theatre to see Jimmy and that it wouldn't matter if he were on the stage by himself. Jimmy had created so many characters over the years that he could easily put them into a three-hour show and people would still come to see him.

This was a point later reinforced by the comments of Marie Jones, the award-winning writer of *Stones in Their Pockets* and *A Night in November* who, as a young actress, had been part of Jimmy's company.

'The function of the rest of the cast was wallpaper,' she stated. 'We knew we were wallpaper. Everybody laughed at him. Nobody laughed at us at all. It was a wonderful feeling being on that stage, listening to all those people and him making them laugh, and turning it on every single night.'

Francie's comments got Jimmy thinking and, a few days later, he approached Jack with the idea of a one-man show which would run for a limited period before the start of their next play. Being a shrewd businessman, Jack immediately saw the benefits of such a show. It could generate the same revenue as a play without the expense of building any sets or paying any other actors. He gave the plan his full support and they set about organising the material that would be required. Jack knew that what Jimmy proposed was a daunting prospect – being alone on the stage for over two hours with no cues from anyone else and no one to help him out. But Jimmy was willing to take the risk.

7

Although Jimmy's new enterprise was to be a one-man show, he knew that it would be impossible to stage without a lot of assistance from behind the scenes. First and foremost, he needed the help of his closest friend.

'Normally, the Group closed down for five weeks in the summer so everyone could have a holiday, but I decided to put the show on then on one condition. I knew that it would need a lot of effects and props, tape recording, background music and lighting changes, and I would only do the show if Jack looked after all of these because I couldn't trust anyone else.'

He also required the assistance of old hands, John Knipe and John McDonnell, to pull together a script. The end result was *Young at Heart*, which opened on 2 August 1966 to a favourable reception. The public loved it and even the normally hostile local critics were generous in their approval. The show played to packed houses for the next two months.

It was a combination of topical material covering current issues, sketches featuring popular characters such as Mrs O'Condriac and Wee Sammy, and more serious monologues. One of the highlights was a comic impression of the Welsh diva, Shirley Bassey. Philip Mulholland explains how Jimmy and Jack devised this part of the show.

The Shirley Bassey sketch was one of Jimmy's funniest and he desperately wanted to include it in *Young at Heart* but, because he could not leave the stage to get into costume in a one-man show, he thought he would have to leave it out.

'Then Jack came up with the idea of a cut out of Shirley's body, minus head and arms, but wearing one of her trademark dresses with big boobs sticking out in front. This was left facing away from the audience in the corner of the stage. When it came time for the sketch, Jimmy took off his jacket, under which he was wearing a shirt without sleeves. As the music started up, he then pulled on a Shirley Bassey wig and, grabbing the cut out from behind, turned round to reveal the woman herself. Then he went into his act.'

Hey Big Spender! Jimmy as Shirley Bassey

Present at one of Jimmy's early solo performances was Mervyn Solomon, the managing director of the local record label, Emerald Records, which was based, in those days, at the end of Ann Street in Belfast. Mervyn recalled his first experience of Jimmy.

'One evening, I was asked to go down and see a comedian perform in the Group Theatre. I sat down in the audience and, after a few minutes, I began to smile. Half an hour later, my sides were bursting. I was

'They have given me my notice, I must pack my bags and go.' Performing the classic monologue, Slum Clearance

introduced to James after the gig and took him to lunch a few days later to discuss the possibility of putting his one-man show together on record.'

Jimmy and Jack gladly accepted Mervyn's offer. Jimmy was magnanimous in his praise for Mervyn, who became a very good friend, and helped a great deal in raising his profile outside Northern Ireland.

'Mervyn Solomon was the biggest recording expert in Ireland and, when the long-playing recordings came about, he was very fair with me over percentages and things. In fact, he was most helpful and generous. I asked him when he wanted me to submit the scripts we would be recording and he said, "Never. If you are doing it, I am happy. I know it will be all right." Mervyn worked tremendously hard to find the best formula and the show that would be best on the record.'

Jimmy had considered pursuing a recording career for many years, going back to the days when he had started working with John Knipe and Tommy James. He loved his record collection and, as well as his favourite singers and musicals, he had a large amount of comic albums from the performers he admired most. These included Ken Dodd, Frankie Howard, Lex McLean, Bob Newhart, Victor Borge, and Tommy Morgan. This last performer was famous for a character by the name of Big Beanie McBride, a Glaswegian version of Orange Lil. Thanks to the opportunity presented by Mervyn Solomon and Emerald Records, Jimmy was now in a position to emulate these great comedians.

To help launch Jimmy's career on vinyl, Mervyn called on the help of Peter Lloyd, a young English sound engineer who had settled in Northern

Peter Lloyd, the sound engineer who helped transfer Jimmy's sell-out shows to bestselling vinyl

An alternative shot of the James Young 4th *album cover*

Ireland after completing his degree at Queen's University. Peter remembers well the recording process behind the first live album.

'Jimmy would always warm up the crowd for maybe ten minutes before the taping started. We made the recordings on a Wednesday evening and a Saturday evening, Wednesday being the country crowd and Saturday being the town crowd. He got different reactions from the two audiences and actually performed differently in front of them. Between the two recordings we would gather the best bits for the album.

'For the first recordings, I used a reel to reel tape recorder and sat in the wings of the Group stage on the left-hand side. I remember once picking up a really annoying laugh through my headphones and it was quite a while before I realised it was actually coming from me.'

The recording of *Young at Heart* proved to be a massive success, selling its initial pressing of 5,000 copies within ten days. It became the first in a series of albums that Jimmy would record over the next five years. These comprised five more one-man shows: *Young and Foolish* (1967), *It's Great*

Receiving the silver disc for achieving 250,000 album sales

to be Young (1968), *James Young 4th* (1969), *James Young – Very Much Live in Canada* (1971), and *The Young Ulsterman* (1973).

Alongside these, Jimmy released three albums of comic songs – *James Young Sings Ulster Party Pieces* (1969), *The Ballymena Cowboy* (1970), and *Behind the Barricades* (1970), as well as six single records for Emerald. The first single, a double A side with *I Protest* and *I'm the Only Catholic on the Linfield Team*, went straight to the top of the local charts in October 1966.

Mervyn Solomon reflected on the phenomenal success of Jimmy's recordings, stating that *Young at Heart* 'became the largest selling (long-playing record) ever by an Irish artist both north and south of the border. James was later presented with a silver disc for selling 250,000 copies. And, in those days, that was an amazing feat.'

While recording the musical tracks for his albums, Jimmy would be in the studio with Peter Lloyd, who remembers him 'smoking away furiously. Then he would start singing along with the backing track. He would get so far before he made a boo-boo and would just say, "Ah f*** it!" So I would have to rewind the tape and start again and he would join in at the spot where he had made the mistake. It took hours and hours to get the song completed but it was always great fun working with him.'

The albums sold worldwide and brought great pleasure to people who had travelled far from the streets of the north. Jimmy acknowledged this fact on the sleeve notes of *It's Great to be Young* where he reproduced some of the fan mail which had been sent from Ulster expatriates in countries as diverse as Canada and South Africa. A letter from a Canadian listener assured Jimmy that he had 'hundreds and hundreds of fans' there, while an Irish writer praised Jimmy for being able 'to bring a better understanding between our peoples than all the politicians put together have achieved in over twenty years'.

Northern Ireland was edging closer to the abyss in 1966. The sectarian and political tensions, which had been simmering for years, were about to boil over with a vengeance, claiming the first three lives of 'the Troubles'. John Scullion, Peter Ward, and Matilda Gould were to lose their lives against a backdrop of mounting social unrest. That year was the 50th anniversary of the Easter Rising but, while commemorative marches and celebrations passed largely without incident, the existing social fabric was beginning to rip apart at the seams.

To unionist alarm, a nationalist candidate, Gerry Fitt, was elected Member of Parliament for West Belfast in the British general election. Unionist Party headquarters were attacked, as were three Catholic schools. A reinvigorated Ulster Volunteer Force issued warnings to the Irish Republican Army (IRA), and the Reverend Ian Paisley established the *Protestant Telegraph* newspaper.

Paisley's star was very much in the ascendancy during this period. Th founder of the Free Presbyterian Church set about organising numerou rallies and street protests to highlight what he and his followers believed t be an imminent sell-out of the state by the then Prime Minister, Terenc O'Neill. These demonstrations led, inevitably, to clashes with nationalist and, eventually, to a prison term for the Reverend.

In his show, Jimmy liked to chat with the audience and crack joke about whatever was newsworthy at the time. As Paisley was most definitel

'No rates in Cherryvalley – only mice.' Jimmy as the Cheeryvalley snob

newsworthy, it wasn't too long before Jimmy introduced a few inoffensive jokes about the fiery orator into his routine. Philip Mulholland remembers well what happened.

'One evening, during the telling of these jokes, Jimmy walked to the edge of the stage and performed a devastating impersonation of the Reverend, in which he allowed his feelings to come to the fore. This absolutely brought the house down. The clapping and laughter seemed to go on and on, so much so that the front of house staff rushed to the balcony to see what was happening. Naturally, Jimmy kept it in the show. Everything went well for the next three or four performances and the impersonation continued to have the audience splitting their sides.

'Unfortunately, it was not to last. During the early performance on the Saturday of the same week, as Jimmy started into his impersonation and moved to the front of the stage, a person suddenly got up from their seat, eight or nine rows back, and hurled a carton of orange juice at Jimmy. It landed at his feet, exploding, and covered the stage and Jimmy's trousers in juice. In shock, he quickly moved to the back of the stage as the culprit and two companions, shouting abuse, left the theatre. At this point, Jack Hudson, who was working the lighting from the wings, walked onstage and had a conversation with Jimmy as loud whispers and murmuring filled the auditorium.

'Jack then returned to the wings as Jimmy, still shaking, walked to the front and picked up the empty carton, making a crack about the fact it was *orange* juice and, to great applause, the show continued.

'That night, Jack urged Jimmy to remove all reference to Paisley from the show but Jimmy refused to be intimidated. A few days later, Jimmy received the first of several threatening phone calls to the theatre. Jack called one of their friends in the Royal Ulster Constabulary but was told there was little they could do. They gave Jimmy the same advice as Jack: drop the impersonation. Jimmy was still reluctant to be intimidated but, after a lot of pleading by Jack and some of Jimmy's close friends, he removed the reference to Ian Paisley from the show. The incident had a lasting effect on Jimmy and was part of the reason he became such an advocate of peace.'

Jimmy's next project was a new play by John McDonnell, *The Wrong Fut*. It opened on 29 November 1966, running for the following seven months. This Galbraith family comedy was quickly succeeded by another one-man show, *Young and Foolish*, a mixture of comedy and pathos which was committed to vinyl and released in time for Christmas 1967. A commercial success, it received high praise from Barry White in the *Belfast Telegraph*, who observed that Jimmy's knack was in picking 'the twin traits of the Ulster character, a weakness for coarseness, such as only a true

Camelot – *in Ballyhalbert!*

puritan can have, and sentimentality. First, the belly laughs then the tears. It's an unbeatable mixture.'

Jimmy had become so well known that it was becoming harder and harder to protect his privacy living in a house so close to the city. He was keen to move to somewhere a little bit more secluded. One evening, while returning from a visit to a couple of Jean Lundy's friends, he spotted a bungalow for sale on the seafront at Ballyhalbert in County Down. He had taken a real liking to the area and was looking to find a property there. Jean tells of how he found his dream house.

Inside Camelot. *Jimmy's chandelier dominates the room*

Welcome to Camelot

'Jimmy was driving through Ballyhalbert when he suddenly brought the car to a stop. "Look, Jean," he said. "That bungalow there, it's for sale."

'So he took a note of the agent and next morning, he was on the phone to them. He was told that yes, it was for sale but no, he couldn't view it because it was let for the month of July. It was apparently let every year for the whole month of July to people who didn't want to be in Belfast over the Twelfth. That was all right and, a few weeks later, as we came out of the theatre one evening, Jimmy said, "Would you take a wee run to Ballyhalbert with me?"

'I said to him, "Are you out of your mind? A wee run to Ballyhalbert? At this time of night? What are you going to Ballyhalbert for?"

'"To have a look at my wee house," he said.

'"Sure, you haven't got that house yet," I said.

'"I know," he said, "but I've put an offer in for it."

'So we went out to see the bungalow and sat outside just admiring it. I hope that those poor people enjoyed that last July in the bungalow, for Jimmy was down every night looking at it. I remember saying to him, "Do you think they're going to set it on fire?"

'Anyway, he got his bungalow eventually and proceeded to tear it apart, redesigning it to his own taste. He made a great job of it too.'

Jimmy named his new home *Camelot* after the Alan Jay Lerner and Frederick Loewe musical. He liked the idea of holding court like King Arthur to all his friends and decided to get a special plaque made, displaying the name at the front of the house. Jean tells the story behind the plaque.

'Jimmy told me he wanted an old-fashioned nameplate for the front of his house with the same lettering that was on the sleeve of his Camelot record. He said, "Jean, I've found a wee man in Hillsborough that works for an ironworks and he makes names for doors. I've sent him up the record sleeve and told him this is what I want."

'Then I said, "You'd be a right looking eedjit if he copies the whole cover with all the cast names. Did you tell him it was just the word Camelot you wanted?"

A portrait shot of Jimmy relaxing at Camelot

"'No, I never thought about that. I just sent him the sleeve and told him this is what I want."

'So I said, "For Gods sake, will you phone the wee man and tell him it's only the one word, Camelot, you want?"'

'And he said, "Ach, I don't know – the whole thing might be nice."'

'Now the record cover was very attractive but I don't think it would have been very suitable hanging over somebody's door.'

Luckily, when the sign arrived, it did only feature the one word and

Clowning around at the Group theatre

Jimmy proudly displayed it at the front of the house, where it remains to this day.

In the context of a fraught political climate, Jimmy continued his success at the Group Theatre by alternating comedy plays, such as *Up the Long Ladder* and *Little Boxes*, with his one-man shows, *It's Great to be Young* and *Comedy Tonight*.

In 1969, Mervyn Solomon approached him with a proposal to tour selected venues in Canada. Mervyn was keen to improve overseas sales of the albums and hoped that live shows for the Ulster ex-pats, many of whom had settled in places like Toronto and Southern Ontario, would generate additional interest.

Jimmy was unsure about taking on such a tour. He was aware that hi brand of comedy might not translate very well abroad, having encountered bad experiences in the past in England and even in Dublin, where the audiences had not warmed to him in the way he would have liked.

But Mervyn Solomon convinced him that the majority of the audience for these shows would be his own countrymen who had emigrated in search of better prospects. After much cajoling, Jimmy eventually agreed and packed his bags for a trip to the New World.

8

Accompanied by Jack Hudson and Mervyn Solomon, Jimmy's short visit to Canada may, in retrospect, be viewed as a trial run for his later, more extensive tour of North America in 1974. While Mervyn was convinced that this first trip could do nothing but good for Jimmy's record sales on the international scene, Jimmy wasn't so sure. In fact, before he set foot on the stage, he was extremely nervous. Jack recalled Jimmy's initial appearance in front of a Toronto audience.

'Jimmy's first "first night" in the New World was a tremendous thrill for him. Back home in Ulster, where he knew and loved his audiences as well as they knew and loved him, he had long ago put the terrors of stage fright behind him. But in this foreign land, among strangers, he was understandably apprehensive. But he need not have worried. As the minutes of his act flew by, the rapport between him and his audience warmed and intensified until, at the end of his performance, the entire audience in the large theatre rose to its feet to give him a standing ovation. The tour lasted just a few weeks and this first response was echoed everywhere Jimmy went. Many members of his audiences were exiled Ulstermen and women and they loved him for the memories he brought them of home. But there were just as many who were not of Ulster extraction who loved him just as much, simply because he was a brilliant comic and a dazzling performer.'

Mervyn Solomon recalled that Jimmy 'seemed to stretch his heart out to the exiles from home.' He also went to great lengths to meet as many of those who had come to see his shows as possible.

'Everywhere he went in Canada he met people from home. The kindness which was shown to him, as a "wee Ulster Man", was quite touching. James had a kind word for everyone and the number of messages he took and passed on to relatives is just an example of the kind heart that he has.'

One of the results of Jimmy's first Canadian adventure was the recording, at the O'Keefe Centre in Toronto, of the bestselling *James Young – Very Much Live in Canada*. The enthusiastic reception of the audience is clear for all to hear on this album, and it isn't surprising to learn that, even before Jimmy had boarded the plane back to Ireland, plans were already being made for his next visit to the land of the maple leaf.

Back in Northern Ireland, Jean Lundy had had a heart attack and was seriously ill in hospital. Informed of this during his tour, Jimmy was very concerned and made a point of calling Jean every night to see how she was keeping. He was unable to cut short his Canadian dates and, despite being the consummate professional, giving his audiences more than their money's worth on stage, his mind became preoccupied with thoughts of getting home to be with his friend. Fortunately, Jean recovered quite quickly from the attack and, on Jimmy's return, he brought her up to *Camelot* to recuperate.

On the phone…

...and applying the greasepaint

Back in his Roddens Park days, Jimmy's housekeeper had been a lady called Mrs Fallis. She was so devoted to him that, when he moved out to Ballyhalbert, she took the long bus trip there from the Braniel estate, where she lived, in order to clean the house for him. Leonard McNeill recalls this lady's dedication.

'Every evening, Jimmy and whoever was down visiting, would sit at the window and wave goodbye to Mrs Fallis as the bus taking her home passed along the road. One evening, about ten minutes after the bus had passed, there was a knock at Jimmy's door. To his amazement, it was Mrs Fallis who, while sitting on the bus, had noticed a streak on one of the windows of the bungalow. She had promptly got off at the next stop and walked back to clean it. She was a quite amazing lady and Jimmy would have been lost without her.'

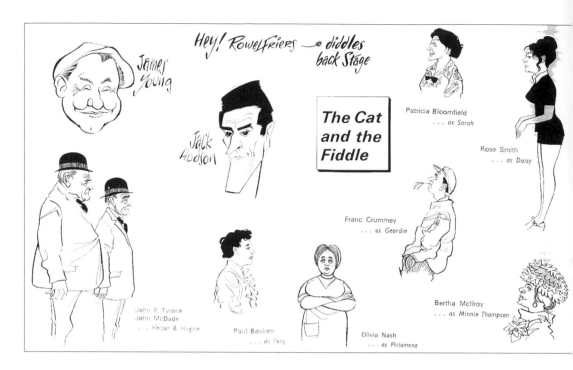

Hey! RowelFriers —• diddles back Stage

James Young

Jack Hodson

The Cat and the Fiddle

Patricia Bloomfield
. . . as Sarah

Rose Smith
. . . as Daisy

Franc Crummey
. . . as Geordie

John F. Tyrone
John McDade
. . . Hector & Hughie

Paul Boskett
. . . as Tony

Olivia Nash
. . . as Philomena

Bertha McIlroy
. . . as Minnie Thompson

Jean also remembers Mrs Fallis as being in possession of quite a sharp tongue.

'One day, I was sitting in Jimmy's back garden when he appeared with a ball of string and a tennis racquet and ball. I think the idea was to cheer me up a bit and give me a laugh. He tied the string across the garden, as if it was tennis netting, and prepared to serve the ball across it. Just then, Mrs Fallis emerged from the back door and announced, "There's someone on the phone for you."

'"Can you not see I'm busy? I'm going to hit this ball over the net," replied Jimmy, jokingly.

'Mrs Fallis retorted, "Sure you couldn't hit a cow's arse with a baking board," and turned on her heels, leaving Jimmy with his ego suitably deflated.'

For the next year-and-a-half, until the spring of 1971, Jimmy continued with his comedy productions (*The Cat and the Fiddle* and *The Dish Ran Away*) and his last solo show at the Group, *Comedy Tonight*. This latter performance was to enter the Guinness Book of Records as the longest run of any one-man show in the world, clocking up 327 performances between 7 April 1969 and 22 March 1970.

Due to Jean Lundy's continuing convalescence, her part in *The Cat and the Fiddle* was filled by a young actress from Larne by the name of Olivia 'Livvy' Nash. Best known now for her part as 'Ma' in the BBC show, *Give My Head Peace*, alongside The Hole in the Wall Gang, Olivia appeared in

Jimmy and Olivia Nash in The Dish Ran Away

all of Jimmy's plays following 1965's *Sticks and Stones*. Speaking today, she is grateful to him for the start he gave her in the acting profession.

'It was a great pleasure to be able to work with Jimmy in the late 60s at the Group. I was very young at the time and it was a great learning experience. Back then, there was no repertory theatre in this country in the same way there was in England. Young people didn't get the same opportunities as they would have had across the water. I was one of the lucky ones and I couldn't give him high enough praise for the way he helped me.'

One of Jimmy's aims during his time at the Group was to provide 'Ulster plays for Ulster audiences' and, with the worsening political situation, he saw his role as providing distraction from the turmoil on the streets. John Keyes maintains that, through his plays, Jimmy genuinely believed he was offering an effective antidote to the poison of sectarianism

'During the beginning part of the Troubles,' says Keyes, '(Jimmy) was very proud of the fact that both Catholics and Protestants came to the Group and sat laughing side by side.'

Similarly, Barry Cowan, who appeared in Jimmy's television series and was later to become one of Northern Ireland's most prominent journalists, states the significance of his shows during the late 60s and early 70s.

'It was great to go and sit in a theatre, or sit in front of your television set, while the rest of the world outside was falling apart and, for an hour or two hours, you could laugh. He was a therapist.'

However, the therapy could only work if the patients could get to their appointments. One of the major problems around this time was that the onslaught of the Troubles had transformed Belfast's city centre into a virtual ghost town outside of normal opening hours. People were sticking to their own homes and areas to minimise the risks of getting caught up in the ongoing conflict. As a result, the bars, restaurants, cinemas and theatres in Northern Ireland's first city experienced a serious slump in trade or went out of business. The Group was no exception.

By 1971, violence was escalating across the North with a corresponding death rate. 180 people were to lose their lives that year against a background of civil disobedience, routine IRA and army gun battles, the calling for a 'Third Force' for loyalism by Ian Paisley and William Craig, and the introduction of internment without trial.

In a year book-ended by the killing of Robert Curtis, the first soldier to die violently during the Troubles, and the bombing of McGurk's bar in Belfast, Jimmy and Jack decided, on 21 May, to close the doors of the Group Theatre. It would be seven years before they opened again, and the two men would not be alive to see it happen.

Since returning from the Middle East together all those years ago, it had been clear to some that Jimmy and Jack had been much more than just friends. At a time when homosexuality was illegal and kept very much from the public gaze, the partners had engaged in a personal relationship but this was to end in the early 60s. From this point on, theirs was, first and foremost, a business partnership and, in their private affairs, both men followed their own paths.

Much has been made of Jimmy's homosexuality but it's probably true to say that, at the very worst, he was a victim of the social norms of his time. Keeping 'in the closet' from fear of alienating his fan base, and finding some sort of release through his gallery of effeminate male characters, he was, for the most part, extraordinarily discreet in his

immy with Paul Boskett, recently graduated from elling programmes at the Group

personal life during and after his romance with Jack.

By the early 70s, however, Jimmy had found a new young partner. This was Paul Boskett, who had joined the staff of the Group in 1968 as a programme seller, but was soon promoted to appearing in small roles in many of Jimmy's productions. Displaying no great penchant for acting, he was, nevertheless, soon playing prominent supporting roles alongside Jimmy onstage.

A lot of young men were regularly to be found in Jimmy's company in those days and, despite suggestions that there was something sordid and sleazy afoot, two of them – Philip Mulholland and Leonard McNeill – state that this was not the case at all. Philip recalls:

*The Jimmy Johnston
Showband*

'In my early teens, as I got to know Jimmy better, I was at no time made
aware that he was involved in any sort of sexual relationships of that
nature. At that time, I was probably his most constant companion, often
attending parties and functions, and accompanying him on trips to
London and Scotland or Dublin.

'Leonard McNeill, who had worked for Jimmy since he was a boy, and
whom Jimmy considered as the son he never had, was by then in his early
twenties, had quit the theatre and fulfilled his dream of becoming a police
officer. He had also recently married a lovely girl, whom Jimmy adored. So
as he spent less and less time with Jimmy, I think that, in some ways,
became a sort of replacement in his eyes.

'I cannot speak of what went on in Jimmy's life before or after I worked
for him. However, I would imagine that, at some time, he and Jack would
have been involved but that side of their relationship was long in the past.
If Jimmy did indulge in any relationships of that kind, he was always
discreet to the point of invisibility.'

Leonard McNeill remembers his friendship with Jimmy as being 'a very
strong platonic relationship. He was a youngster at heart and he had to
surround himself with young people.' In short, Jimmy was 'young at heart
as well as Young in name'.

Closing the Group Theatre, Jimmy's theatrical home for over ten years,
had been an incredibly difficult decision to make. The truth was, of course
that declining audiences had made it no longer financially viable to run.
By a stroke of luck, however, another avenue opened up from an unlikely
source.

In the 1960s and early 70s, many showbands toured all over Ireland playing pubs and clubs and other small venues. One such band was the Jimmy Johnston Showband, which had scored a few hits such as *The Pub with No Beer* and *My Son Calls Another Man Daddy*, released by Emerald Records.

Two key members of the band, Jimmy Johnston himself and Maurice Beckett, who played keyboard and trumpet, had branched out and formed a small agency called JB Promotions. They were based in High Street, Belfast, and arranged bookings for bands at the various venues around the country.

In early 1971, St Coleman's Hall in Derry approached the agency to enquire as to whether James Young would be available to perform at a gala show they were staging. Maurice Beckett called the Group Theatre and asked Jack if Jimmy could perform in Derry that evening. It transpired that Jimmy could, indeed, do a late-night one-man show after his performance was finished at the Group. With this bit of good fortune, St Coleman's arranged their programme so that the gala show would start at 8pm with a few supporting acts, followed by Jimmy providing the headline entertainment at 10.30pm. Maurice Beckett recounts what happened next.

'A few days later, I got a call from Jack Hudson saying that, instead of Jimmy just coming on at the very end of the show, they could cancel that evening's performance of the current play at the Group. Jimmy could come onstage at 8pm and do his whole one-man show, and St Coleman's Hall wouldn't have to book any other artists. So that's what happened and, of course, the place was a total sell out.'

After this, JB Promotions became Jimmy's official booking agents and began organising shows for him at various spots around the country. As this new development coincided with the decision to close the Group, it helped to soften the blow somewhat and provided an alternative form of income. Jimmy now had the freedom to travel around and perform at virtually any type of venue. In an interview with *City Week* journalist, John Trew, Jimmy borrowed a famous line from the actress, Mrs Patrick Campbell, when he declared, 'My show, as you know, has always been a *tour de force* – now I'm forced to tour.'

Jimmy at Antrim's Steeple Inn

THE STEEPLE INN, Antrim presents: Thurs., Fri., Sat.,
THE JAMES YOUNG SHOW

Music by CANDIDA
Admission at door

Since, with the Troubles kicking in, people were less likely to go to the theatre, Jimmy was determined to take the theatre to the people. He played anywhere and everywhere – town halls, cabaret clubs, bars, schools, and hospitals – any place he could get an audience assembled. He played in many of the popular cabaret spots of the day, such as the Abercorn in Belfast's Cornmarket and the Steeple Inn in Antrim. He also performed at cinemas and any theatres that had remained opened, such as the Grove Theatre on Belfast's Shore Road.

Ulster 71, where Jimmy stole the limelight with his marathon run of shows

Jimmy's shows were a combination of comic patter and serious monologues, ranging from an X-rated skit on the popular children's television show, *Romper Room*, to a rendition of the evergreen *Slum Clearance*. Changing the content of each show in tune with the demands of each audience, he would provide two-and-a-half hours of typical James Young entertainment. Right from his opening quip – 'It's great to be here. Me Mammy's had me ready since dinnertime' – Jimmy would have the audiences eating out of his hands.

One of the highlights of the year was his marathon run of shows at the *Ulster 71* exhibition in Belfast's Stranmillis grounds. Starting at 2pm, Jimmy did eight performances, finishing at 11pm, with a strange plastic balloon enclosure doubling as the 'theatre'.

Jack was later to reflect on Jimmy's early 70s shows and the different venues he played.

'Despite the Troubles, Jimmy was able to take his humour, with its strong and often quite controversial political content, into every part of

Northern Ireland without being threatened for his views and opinions. He relied, as he always had done, on the basic good nature of people and their ability to laugh at themselves. The warmth which greeted him everywhere extended to those who went with him, with the result that I was probably the only Englishman, and an ex-member of the British Army to boot, who had been into and out of the Bogside in Derry without a large bodyguard of soldiers. In one week, we played exactly the same show, with exactly the same jibes at all the politicians, in the Loyalist Club on the Shankill Road and the Community Centre in the Bogside. And they got exactly the same laughter from the two audiences.'

Jimmy himself made his feelings clear about religion.

'The saddest thing about religion in this country,' he said, 'is the way people let it influence their attitudes to others. As far as I'm concerned, I don't give a "tuppeny bun" what particular faith anyone follows. They're all human beings to me.

'Somebody once told me that there were things I've said on stage that would have got me stoned up the Shankill or the Falls, but I disagreed. Belfast has an ability to laugh at itself, even though some past events would seem to contradict that.'

The cabaret days brought Jimmy even closer to his audience, as Jack observed, singling out Jimmy's ability 'to create the illusion he was talking straight to you… After a two-and-a-half-hour solo performance, he never allowed anyone to know what an effort it could be to stand and sign autographs.'

Indeed, Jimmy's philosophy concerning autographs was: 'I'll start worrying when they stop asking me.'

Incredibly, despite this proven popularity, there were still some theatre and nightclub proprietors who turned down the opportunity to stage Jimmy's show. Maurice Beckett singles out a venue manager in Newcastle, County Down, who balked at Jimmy's fee. To prove how popular a draw he was, JB Promotions hired the venue themselves and staged the show. Beckett recalls:

'So we rented the place out, and that night, hours before the show started, the crowds were queued right the way out of Newcastle town. (The owner), of course, was raging about this and, when we asked him to open

Backstage, gathering his thoughts after a show at the Alpha Cinema

the balcony for us to let more people in, he very pettily refused. Anyway the next day we got a phone call from (him), asking if he could book Jimmy in a fortnight's time… But we just said no. He had missed his chance.'

Jimmy even ventured over the border on occasion. Dessie McKeown who had been appointed road manager to Jimmy at this time, remember a misunderstanding at a performance in Dundalk.

'James got to the part of the show were he launched into one of his most famous monologues, *I Loved a Papish*. It started off, "I was born and bred in Sandy Row, a loyal Orange Prod. A follower of King William, that noble man of god". No sooner had James recited those lines when a man stood, bolt upright, in the middle of one of the front rows and made his way to the exit where I was sitting.

'"Do you want a pass out, sir?" I asked.

'"No, I do not!" he replied. He then said, "I don't know where you get those bloody Protestants from," as he stormed out. If he had sat on, he would have realised the theme of the monologue was the sort of religious intolerance he was displaying.'

Another time, Jack Hudson was unwell and Jimmy asked Leonard McNeill to accompany him to a show in Buncrana to operate the sound system. Leonard agreed and everything went well until the end of the evening, when he inadvertently left the tape machine running while talking to Jimmy. The next thing, the opening bars of *God Save the Queen* started playing through the hall speakers. Leonard sprang into action.

'I don't think I have ever moved as fast in my life. I rushed over as quickly as I could and managed to get the thing turned off. The caretaker of the theatre approached me and asked what the problem was and, after I

Jimmy and Paul, backstage, at the Alpha Cinema, Rathcoole, 1972

told him, he said, "Ach sure, we don't worry about that sort of thing over here."

'But I noticed a few unsavoury glances from other members of the audience and was very glad when we made our exit.'

No matter how far away the venue for the evening show was, Jimmy and Jack always travelled back at night so that Jimmy could get home to his beloved *Camelot*. Jack owned a luxury flat on the Malone Road in Belfast and, when Jimmy set off each evening, he would drive up to Jack's place, leave his car there, and Jack would drive him to the show in his Bentley.

One night, they played in Derry and it was about 2am before Jimmy left Jack's house in his own car to travel the 25 miles along the coast to Ballyhalbert. About two miles from his house, he was stopped at an army checkpoint and asked by the soldiers to show them his driving licence. Jimmy never carried a licence, assuming that he was very easy to recognise. Unfortunately, Jimmy's fame had not yet reached the part of England that these young soldiers hailed from.

Requesting that Jimmy open the boot of his car, the soldiers were met with a weird and wonderful assortment of women's clothing, several bizarre wigs, and a nasty looking First World War bayonet. This find, coupled with their late night driver's inability to produce proper identification, convinced the soldiers that something was amiss.

Jimmy, given the contents of his car boot, didn't see how he could possibly fit their picture of a terrorist and made several attempts to reason with the soldiers. A battered old letter addressed to him at the Group Theatre didn't convince them and, unfortunately, there were no RUC personnel present who might have recognised him.

Jimmy's temper soon got the better of him. He was tired and cold and had had a very long day. He protested that he wasn't going to stand around all night. Desperately trying to think of anyone who might be able to vouch for him, he told one of the soldiers, equipped with a radio set, to 'ask the Prime Minister. I was talking with him today.'

After contemplating how the cross-dressing, unidentified suspicious character standing in front of him could possibly have been conversing with Northern Ireland's Prime Minister, the soldier gave it a shot.

Speaking to the operator back at base, the soldier began, 'I've got a man here, who says he lives in Ballyhalbert. He wears women's clothing and says he knows the Prime Minister. And he's got a 14 inch weapon in his car.'

The confusion over Jimmy's apparent threat to national security was soon resolved and the soldiers let him get on his way. Despite his ordeal Jimmy offered to make the squaddies some coffee. The offer was obviously very welcome.

'How many shall I bring up?' asked Jimmy, looking around at the three of them.

'Fourteen,' was the reply. The rest of the platoon suddenly emerged from behind a hedge where they had been covering Jimmy with their rifles.

On arriving home, Jimmy made several large flasks of coffee. He brought these, along with a packet of biscuits and all the cups and beakers he could muster, back down the road in a cardboard box. Pointing out his house to the soldiers, he asked them to leave the box and contents on his doorstep when they were finished. Jack Hudson explained what happened next.

'When Jimmy got up in the morning, he went to the door for the crockery, but no cups, no flasks, no box! Damning the entire British Army, he drank his morning coffee from a milk jug. Later in the day he learned that, at eight o'clock that morning, the RUC and army had been called to his neighbour's house, together with the bomb disposal squad, to investigate a mysterious cardboard box, which had been left outside.

'One can imagine the chagrin of the intrepid soldier who opened it up, only to find Jimmy's dirty crockery. And their feelings when they found out that the army had caused its own bomb scare.'

Jimmy playing the mannequin for two admirers at the 1973 Ideal Home Exhibition

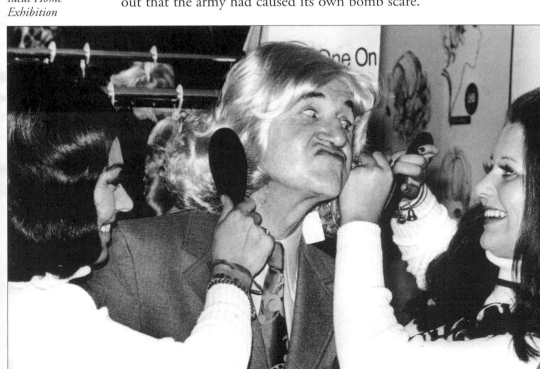

The long journeys around the province began to prove very wearying for Jimmy. He was glad, therefore, when at the start of 1972, the BBC offered him the chance to star in his own television series.

The idea of a television show had been discussed since the mid-60s but, for one reason or another, the project had never materialised. That was all about to change, however, as Jimmy prepared to give his comic creations a new lease of life – in front of the camera.

9

By the time the first episode of Jimmy's new television show, *Saturday Night*, had finished transmitting on 14 October 1972, the 643rd life had been snuffed out in the Troubles.

This is important to remember, as is the fact that the show premiered towards the end of what had been, and still is to this day, the most violent year of the conflict. Bloody Sunday and Bloody Friday, the imposition of direct rule from London, and the spilling over of violence on to the British 'mainland' were some of the events that cluttered the news headlines. This added to the already palpable sense of despair amongst people who could see no end to the spiralling nightmare.

Given this context, Jimmy sought, through his sketches, songs and monologues to offer a distraction for people from the crisis on the streets. The show was a resounding success, achieving more than respectable viewing figures and even prompting critics to set aside their traditional begrudgery to applaud the marriage of Jimmy's talent to BBC Northern Ireland's technical resources.

Jimmy's colourful collection of characters, honed and perfected over many years, made their debut on television screens across the land, cheering up the populace between the dreaded news bulletins, which always seemed to bring word of yet another atrocity or loss of life.

Jimmy in the 'wee street'

The 'wee street' inhabited by Derek and his Mammy, Emily and Willie Beattie, Mrs O'Condriac, Orange Lil, Billy Hulk, and Big Sadie harked back to days when there was no Troubles and, if there were problems, they really didn't matter that much. Keyholders were not asked to return to their premises to check for incendiary devices. A knock at the front door was nothing more

Jimmy launching Northern Ireland's senior citizen holiday scheme in 1972, flanked by two admiring fans

suspicious or threatening than a neighbour asking for a cup of sugar. And Catholics and Protestants inhabited the same rows of terrace houses, not having yet been dispersed to live among their 'own kind'.

It was, in the words of critic Ian Hill, 'an affectionate picture of a cosy urban society that probably never existed'. Issues such as sectarianism, discrimination, unemployment, poverty, and so on, were touched on in the show, but in an affectionate, reassuring, never controversial, manner. The series struck a chord and, where the alternative was to wallow in the doom and gloom of what had become everyday life to local people, it offered something positive, familiar and cheering. Every Saturday night, at the end of an hour or so, it was with Jimmy's plea – 'Will yis, for God's sake, stop fightin'?' – echoing in their ears that many viewers chose to go to their beds.

Jimmy and Jack with Saturday Night *producer, George Hewardine*

The man behind the scenes on the *Saturday Night* series was producer George Hewardine. Alongside his film director, Matt Carruth, George would gather the principal cast – Jimmy, Jack, Jean and Paul Boskett – in one of the little side streets, off Dublin Road, for location filming every Tuesday morning. This was the site for the 'wee street' in the show. Jean recalls that 'a woman cleared her house, and let us have it for filming. That would be Derek's house, where he lived with his Mammy. Next door would be where Emily and Willie Beattie lived.'

These location pieces would be interspersed with live material, which was recorded a couple of hours before the show was due to be broadcast. According to Jean, the scripts for the live segments would be sent up on the Enterprise train from Dublin on Saturday mornings, leaving very little time to rehearse before going out in front of the studio audience. Jimmy used to go through the scripts as he drove her to the BBC in Belfast.

'I honestly don't know how we weren't both killed,' she says, 'for Jimmy paid more attention to learning his lines than he did driving the car.'

To add to the pressure, Jean remembers that 'Jimmy would constantly change the lines and not get on his marks for the camera. That hadn't mattered at the Group but it was very important in live television. I felt sorry for those poor cameramen, for they had to follow him about, trying to get the right shot. George Hewardine was a real gentleman and he had the patience of Job. He had a way of handling Jimmy and it all came together in the end.'

Jimmy and Jean as Big Derek and Emily in the BBC Saturday Night show

Jimmy as the model neighbour, Mrs O'Condriac

Jean also tells a story of how undergarments were procured for one of Jimmy's most popular characters.

'When Jimmy was playing Mrs O'Condriac, he had the famous old black coat on but, anytime he was getting up from a chair or climbing into cars, he always made sure the audience saw these big wide knickers with the elastic legs he had on. Now one of my jobs was going out to buy these big knickers for him.

'So one day, myself and another female cast member, went down to Arnott's in town to get some more of them. We went into the shop and I said to the assistant, who was this rather elderly lady, "I would like a pair of large outsize fleece knickers."

Emily Beattie's Auntie - counting those pennies

'"No problem," she said, and went down the back of the shop and brought some out.

'I held them up to the girl I was with and she asked, "Do you think he would like those? Are they the colour he wants?"

'"Ach," I said. "Jimmy would wear any colour."

'The assistant couldn't quite believe what she was hearing and she asked us, "Are these for *a man*?"

'She obviously hadn't seen the show, or recognised me, and thought that something very peculiar was going on.'

BBC Broadcasting House staff were kept very busy throughout the show's run, dealing with requests for tickets and answering the fan mail.

Hundreds of letters and Christmas cards were sent from viewers, thanking Jimmy and the BBC for cheering them up during this bleakest of periods. When the series came to an end, the BBC immediately commissioned a St Patrick's Day special with Jimmy and the gang.

With a top rated television show, a successful recording career and a cabaret act that sold out at every venue, Jimmy was at the peak of his game. To maintain all of this, however, required a phenomenal amount of hard work. Now aged 54, Jimmy pushed himself on, trying to keep up with it all. Eventually, his body just couldn't take any more.

On 2 April 1973, Jack Hudson received a telephone call from Newtownards Hospital.

'Jimmy had been taken ill. When I got to the hospital, he was in the intensive care unit, being monitored by the electronic apparatus for a heart condition. Apparently, he had felt ill as he was driving through Greyabbey and sensibly called in with his doctor, who lives there. The doctor had, at once, suspected heart trouble and had him taken to Newtownards. It was whilst he was in hospital that he had the heart attack.

'Knowing Jimmy so well, I informed the newspapers that he had a virus infection, and that he hoped to be well enough to leave hospital in a short while.'

After a few days, Jimmy felt quite well again. His doctor advised him to remain in hospital for a few weeks and take a complete rest at home afterwards. The doctor also insisted that Jimmy quit smoking and lose some weight. Jimmy had been a smoker since his teens but, with a great amount of willpower, he managed to give the cigarettes up completely. He also went on a diet and lost three-and-a-half stone in weight, changing his physical appearance quite dramatically.

THE ULSTER SOCIETY OF EDMONTON

ANNUAL

ST. PATRICK'S CELEBRATION BALL

HOLLAND HOUSE
12940 - 127 Street, Edmonton
SATURDAY, MARCH 16, 1974

COCKTAILS 6:00 P.M. - GRAND MARCH AND BANQUET 7:15 P.M.

REFRESHMENTS · ENTERTAINMENT · DOOR PRIZES

Dress Semi-Formal
Everyone Welcome

$10.00 Per Person
Dancing 9:00 p.m. - 2:00 a.m.

Nº 195

Nº 195

Invitation to the Ulster Society's St Patrick's Celebration Ball in Edmonton

Jimmy at the Ebell Wishire Theatre in Hollywood

For the rest of that spring and summer, Jimmy stayed at *Camelot*, taking the exercise prescribed by the doctor and keeping to his rigid diet. He had more time to entertain his friends and look after his garden, which he enjoyed tremendously, but the enforced rest soon made him itchy to start work again.

Jack had a consultation with the medical people who advised that Jimmy could work if he wished to, but only if it was restricted to a fraction of what it had been before.

Jack soon found out that getting Jimmy to cut down was an enormous problem. Arrangements had been made to cut out all cabaret work if Jimmy was working on his television show and, at other times, the cabarets would be restricted to a maximum of three in any one week. This was all very well until Jack found out, time after time, that Jimmy had agreed to do 'a little talk' to this or that society in his free time.

Nevertheless, after a few weeks, Jimmy underwent another medical examination and was pronounced very fit. Indeed, he was feeling better than he had for some years.

One morning around Christmas 1973, Jimmy was awakened at 2am by a telephone call from Sam Donaghey, the President of the Ulster Society in Toronto. He asked Jimmy if he would provide the cabaret spot at the St Patrick's Eve ball in Edmonton. Jimmy was already engaged by the BBC to make programmes right up to, and including, St Patrick's Day in 1974 but, with a bit of pre-recording he was able to commit to the trip to Canada.

Initially, Jack was apprehensive about Jimmy making such a long journey. As it happened, however, his second North American visit was organised in such a way that he would have plenty of time for rest between engagements.

Edmonton's Ulster Society awarded him for his outstanding endeavour in the field of Irish entertainment and human relations. The warmth of his welcome from the Irish community in the city left him in no doubt that this was no token award, but came from their hearts.

After a week's sightseeing in Vancouver, Jimmy did three nights at an Irish club called *The Blarney Stone*, before driving down the California coast to Hollywood. It was here that he played for one night at the Ebell Wilshire Theatre. Jack noted how the three-hour show in front of an audience of nearly 2,000 went down.

'I have seen him give many thousands of performances, and never once a bad one; but that night, he must have given the finest of his life. It had always been the ambition of his life to play Hollywood, the Mecca of the entertainment world, and he left his highly sophisticated and extremely critical audience in no doubt that he was a great performer, a master of his art.'

A Belfast comedian playing to a packed theatre in the world's movie capital was a definite first and he brought the house down. Jimmy took three curtain calls, was given a standing ovation and was accorded just about every honour, short of the freedom of Los Angeles. The function also raised over $2,000 for the Mary Peters Track Fund.

The show had been organised by two Ulstermen living in Los Angeles, John Rickerby and Bill Cunningham. Rickerby commented at the time that 'half of the audience were Ulster expatriates but the rest were people from Los Angeles, who had never heard or seen him before, and they loved him.'

He concluded: 'The Ulster people over here have had little to be proud of these past few years. After this, we are all walking a little taller.'

From Hollywood, Jimmy and Jack flew to Toronto for some more shows and a television appearance on Global TV with Bernard Braden. Finally, they travelled to Detroit for a reception by the Irish American Club, at which Jimmy was presented with the key to the city. Over a seven-week period, Jimmy had only given eight performances and, despite a lot of travelling, had managed to relax during a large part of his tour.

Back at home, Jimmy rang Jack one mid-June morning to tell him that there had been mysterious inquiries being made about his date of birth. Jimmy usually laughed off questions about his age by joking, 'Sure, I've been 39 for the past ten years and I'm not going to change now.'

Jack's theory about these inquiries was that Jimmy was probably being nominated for inclusion in the New Year's honours list. It transpired that Jack was correct. Jimmy was due to honoured with an MBE at the start of 1975. However, events dictated that this was not to be.

Friday 5 July 1974 started off much like any other day. Jimmy called Jean, who had just returned from a holiday in Cornwall with her husband, Teddy. Jimmy had been invited to Jean's home that evening for a meal and was checking the arrangements. He informed her that he would be attending the funeral of Paul Boskett's grandmother that day, after he had fulfilled a previously agreed engagement, acting as a judge in a Northern Ireland Tourist Board contest.

Attending the Northern Ireland Tourist Board competition lunch on the day of his death

'What's the contest about?' asked Jean.

'It's a contest to say why you would take your holidays in

Bangor,' replied Jimmy. 'If someone asked you, what would you say?'

'I would take my holidays in Bangor just to sit on the oil drums!' Jean joked, explaining later that, for security reasons, 'back then, they had oil drums in front of nearly every shop in Bangor. How they would prevent a bomb blast getting through, I don't know, since the gap between them was wide enough for a horse and cart.'

Both friends said their goodbyes, agreeing that they would see each other that evening.

Jimmy spent the morning as one of a team of judges in the Northern Ireland Tourist Board's Budget Breakaways Holiday Competition. Billy Hastings, of the Hastings Hotel Group, was also one of the judges. He remembers that Jimmy 'had a grey appearance' that day.

'He didn't star at the table. He spoke when spoken to … and I felt that, in itself, to be quite strange because he was always very ebullient and effervescent.'

When speaking to Roberta Wallace, a local reporter for the *Belfast Telegraph*, at the same event, Jimmy seemed to have got some of his old sparkle back. Roberta wrote:

'He seemed his normal amusing self, and was full of jokes about Ulster boarding houses and the characters found in the tourist industry. He told me that he was booked to do another tour of Canada, starting mid-September, and he was looking forward to seeing all the Ulster exiles once again.'

At about 1pm, after the judging was finished, Jimmy returned to his car and changed his tie for a black one. He drove a cream P1800 Volvo Sports Coupe, a very distinctive vehicle at that time, as Roger Moore had one in the popular television show, *The Saint*.

He started his journey to Carnmoney, in Glengormley, where the funeral was taking place, accompanied by his pet dog, a little stray jokingly named Edna. This name came from the lead character in a BBC play, *Edna the Inebriate Woman*, and quickly stuck because the dog had a bit of a strange walk, making it look like it was permanently drunk.

Jimmy cut through the town, on to the Shore Road, which would bring him all the way to Newtownabbey. He had played at the Grove Theatre on the Shore Road just a fortnight before and, on opening night, had presented Mary Peters with a cheque for the money raised at his Hollywood concert.

As he approached the Grove, Jimmy began to feel unwell. He pulled his car over to the side of the road.

A little while later, at her home in Crawfordsburn, Jean was preparing to leave for the hairdressing salon when the telephone rang. It was George Hewardine.

'Have you been talking to Jimmy today?' he asked.

'Of course,' Jean informed him. 'Jimmy phones me every day of his life.'

'There's rumours that he's had an accident on the Shore Road, and he may be dead.'

'Ach, no,' said Jean. 'Jimmy's going to a funeral up the Shore Road today. Somebody's got mixed up. It's amazing how these rumours get around.'

George agreed that that was probably the case. Jean hung up the telephone and left to have her hair done.

By this time, a pedestrian on the Shore Road had called the emergency services to a car parked at the kerb with the driver apparently slumped at the wheel. When the police arrived, Leonard McNeill was informed that they were prevented from getting too close to Jimmy because of his overly protective dog. Edna snapped and barked in an attempt to keep the strangers away from her master.

'The local police had a terrible job getting in,' Leonard recalls. 'They were afraid of being eaten by the dog.'

After Edna was removed, the cardiac crew frantically tried to revive Jimmy, but it was too late. After he had pulled the car over, he'd suffered a massive coronary and died on the spot. The medical team pronounced him dead at the scene and his body was removed to the mortuary at Laganbank Road.

Jean remembers how she came to hear the terrible news.

'When I walked into the hairdresser's, the owner said to me, "Isn't it terrible about Mr Young?"

'I said, "What about him?" And she told me what she had just heard on the news.

'It was then I realised the awful truth. I just turned and walked out of the place. From that day to this, I don't know where I went after that. I was just in a daze, in complete and utter shock.'

Frank Crummey was later to comment: 'Jimmy always said that the one fear he had was dying in the street. Sadly, that's exactly what happened.'

On 5 July 1974, at approximately 3pm, in the shadow of Belfast's Grove Theatre, James Young died. He was 56 years old.

10

As Jimmy's body left *Camelot* in Ballyhalbert on Tuesday 9 July 1974, dozens of local people lined the seafront road. Jack Hudson and Jimmy's surviving sisters, May Young and Peggy McKay, followed solemnly behind.

Jimmy's next-door neighbour, Vera Guest, wept as she watched the funeral from the side of her bungalow.

'He was much loved down here,' she said. 'People used to call him the Lord Mayor of Ballyhalbert.'

The cortege left Ballyhalbert and headed up the coast, through Greyabbey, and on to Newtownards. It then passed through Dundonald, heading for Belfast. All along the route, police stopped traffic to allow the procession through. As it entered the predominantly Protestant east Belfast, housewives on the Newtownards Road gathered in small groups to watch. Men stood outside pubs, surveying the scene, and workers downed tools as a mark of respect.

Passing along May Street, in the Catholic Markets area, a group of locals blessed themselves as the coffin went by, with some women openly weeping.

It was 2pm when the funeral procession reached the Group Theatre in Bedford Street, the place where Jimmy had brought so much joy and laughter to so many. On numerous occasions, he'd had his audiences in tears with his poignant monologues, and the tears flowed again on this saddest of days. Fans had queued up at the theatre, as they had to see his shows, to bid their favourite star farewell.

Among the wreaths sitting outside the Group was one from the cast members of *The McCooeys*, the show that had started Jimmy on his rise to fame. Outside the theatre, a poster for *The Dish Ran Away* was still on display. This was the last play Jimmy had starred in before the venue's doors had been forced to close.

The cortege stopped outside the Group. Jack Hudson emerged from one of the vehicles and walked alone behind the hearse as it travelled

Queuing outside the Group Theatre on 9 July 1974 to watch 'Our Jimmy' make his final journey

around the corner to the BBC in Ormeau Avenue. Travelling up the Ormeau Road, past the streets where Jimmy had spent his childhood years, on by Braniel and Roddens Park, where he had lived for a large part of his adult life, the funeral finally reached Roselawn crematorium, which was packed to capacity with close friends and acquaintances.

Among the mourners gathered were Joseph Tomelty, J G Devlin, Sam Cree and Harold Goldblatt. They had worked alongside Jimmy many times and had come to pay their final respects to their friend.

The Reverend Ian Patterson, rector of the Church of the Holy Redeemer, conducted the short service. Derek Marsden, who had been Jimmy's musical director for some years, provided accompaniment on the church organ, playing two of Jimmy's favourite hymns: *The Lord is My Shepherd* and *Mine Eyes Have Seen the Glory of the Coming of the Lord*.

Fittingly, Jack gave the eulogy.

'It is most appropriate that, on the most solemn and final occasion in the life of Jimmy Young, he had, as usual, a capacity audience,' he began. 'The only ingredient missing today is the sound of laughter and, that too, is appropriate. Not because of the nature of the day but because very little of the vast repertoire of words he used on stage were funny, unless delivered with that unmistakeable voice, the mischievous facial expression, the eloquence of his gestures and, above all, the superb timing of his delivery.

Order of Service

FOR

JAMES YOUNG

ROSELAWN CREMATORIA

TUESDAY, 9th JULY, 1974

The Service will be conducted by
Rev. I. F. R. PATTERSON, B.A:

Organist: DEREK MARSDEN

THE PROCESSIONAL
(The Congregation is requested to stand)

HYMN

THE Lord's my shepherd, I'll not want,
He makes me down to lie
In pastures green; he leadeth me
The quiet waters by.

My soul he doth restore again,
And me to walk doth make
Within the paths of righteousness,
E'en for his own name's sake.

Yea, though I walk in death's dark vale
Yet I will fear no ill
For though art with me, and thy rod
And staff me comfort still.

My table thou hast furnished
In presence of my foes;
My head thou dost with oil anoint
And my cup overflows.

Goodness and mercy all my life,
Shall surely follow me
And in God's house for evermore
My dwelling place shall be.

A READING FROM THE NEW TESTAMENT
1st Corinthians 15, verse 20

EULOGY BY JACK HUDSON

HYMN

Mine eyes have seen the glory of the coming of the Lord;
He is trampling out the vintage where the grapes of wrath are stored;
He hath loosed the fateful lightning of his terrible swift sword:
His truth is marching on.

Glory, Glory, Hallelujah, Glory, Glory, Hallelujah,
Glory, Glory, Hallelujah, His truth is marching on.

He hath sounded forth the trumpet that shall never call retreat;
He is sifting out the hearts of men before his judgement seat;
O be swift, my soul, to answer him; be jubilant my feet!
Our God is marching on!

In the beauty of the lillies our Christ was born across the sea,
With Glory in His bosom that transfigures you and me;
As he died to make men holy, let us live to make men free,
While God is marching on.

He is coming like the glory of the morning on the wave;
He is wisdom to the mighty; He is succour to the brave;
So the world shall be his footstool and the soul of time his slave:
Our God is marching on.

THE CREED

THE PRAYERS

THE COMMITTAL

THE LORD'S PRAYER

THE BLESSING

The service card for Jimmy's funeral

'A true perfectionist of his art, his greatest fulfilment came with the waves of affectionate laugher during a comedy, or the utter silence during the beautifully judged dramatic pauses in a serious monologue.

'I was very proud, not only in seeing him honoured across the Atlantic, but in seeing what a good ambassador he was for this country, which he loved so much. Indeed, I can best illustrate Jimmy's passionate faith in his fellow countrymen by quoting you from his final speech, which he made after every performance, in all parts of Ireland, over the past four years and, indeed, used only the night before his death.

'"This little country of ours has become renowned throughout the world for its violence and hatred but, wherever I go, I try to tell them about the people they do not hear about. I tell them that when people of different religions and politics can sit together and laugh and cry at things we have laughed and cried about, here tonight, there can be little wrong with their spirit and, someday, that spirit will solve all our troubles."

'That was the message he took to America and, I trust someday, his faith will be proven right.'

Rowel Friers, the renowned *Belfast Telegraph* cartoonist, who had drawn numerous caricatures of Jimmy for theatre programmes, personalised invitations and Christmas cards, attended the funeral and was struck by the big turnout of local celebrities from the stage and small screen. Indeed, there was a certain theatrical air about the funeral. Rowel recalled that, as Jimmy's coffin was being lowered for cremation, he turned to the person beside him and whispered: 'I bet you it comes up for an encore.'

Later that day, Jack collected Jimmy's ashes and started to think about his own future. With Jimmy gone, he had no real reason to stay in Northern Ireland and soon decided to emigrate to Canada. During one of their trips there together, he and Jimmy had been offered the opportunity to start a theatre in Edmonton, a city which, surprisingly, didn't have one of its own. Jimmy had asked Jean Lundy to accompany them.

'What about my husband, Teddy?' enquired Jean.

'Sure, he can come too,' Jimmy replied. 'We'll need an accountant for the new theatre.'

'Go and boil your head,' was Jean's response. 'If you think I'm leaving the rest of my family to go to the other side of the world, you've got another thing coming.'

That had put the idea on hold for a while.

When Jimmy's will was read, he, not unexpectedly, left everything to Jack. The will had been written in 1962 and Jimmy had never seen the need to change it. There was little else Jack could do but sell up and move on. He put *Camelot* on the market and gave away or sold those possessions of Jimmy's which he could not transport to Canada.

Before he left, Jean asked him, 'Are you not telling your family in London that you're emigrating, Jack?'

'There are only three people in this world who care if I live or die,' he replied, 'and that's you, Teddy and Lorraine.' Lorraine was Jean's daughter.

With that, Jack Hudson left Northern Ireland for the very last time.

A short time after Jimmy's death, plans were put forward to build a new theatre in his honour. When Jack became aware of this, he wrote a letter to a local newspaper. In it, he said that, while the project was commendable, Jimmy would not have wanted this honour. Instead, he declared, 'if it is the wish of the people to perpetuate his memory, in tangible form, the ending of violence would be all that he desired.'

Jack concluded the letter by writing:

'I know that, for myself, not a day passes but that I think of him and, so often in my new life in the theatre in Edmonton, Alberta, his example and his genius inspire me in my work. I, therefore, hope, as I know he would wish, that no one attempts to copy his work, or live in the past, or perpetuate something that has ended. He often remarked, when he heard a new discovery described as a second Judy Garland or a second Frank Sinatra, or whoever: "How much better to be a *first* John Smith".'

Jack's new life in Canada was, sadly, not to last. On Tuesday 7 June 1977, friends from the Edmonton theatre became concerned when he didn't show up for a meeting. He was such a punctual person that, when he didn't appear, someone was sent from the theatre to check on him. When they were unable to gain access to his flat, the police were called. Eventually, they managed to gain access and found Jack dead on the bathroom floor. He was 54 years old.

That same day, Jean Lundy and her husband, Teddy, had driven from Scotland to Land's End to see the bonfire there being lit in honour of the Queen's Silver Jubilee. On their return to the hotel in Newquay, the couple was confronted by an excited manager, who informed Jean that the Canadian police had been trying to contact her. When he further explained that it had been the vice squad looking for her, Teddy began to wonder what Jean had been up to that he didn't know about.

However, the manager then explained that 'a Mr Hudson has been found dead in his apartment.'

Jean remembers that, on hearing the news, she nearly dropped dead herself.

'Something I didn't know,' Jean now points out, 'was that Jack had said in his will that, in the event of his death, I was to be notified.'

Jean's presence was required in Edmonton, and Teddy and herself began the long journey back to Scotland that very night in order to fly from there to Canada.

'It was a difficult trip,' she says, 'trying to keep Teddy awake on the long drive from Cornwall, on a very bad stormy night. Then things were complicated even more by the fact that I fell and broke my ankle coming out of an all-night travel stop on the way up. Jimmy could have written a play about it.'

Complete with her ankle in plaster, Jean boarded a plane the next day. Due to business commitments, Teddy was unable to accompany her, and she found herself pondering what awaited her at the end of what she now refers to as 'a long, weary, worrying journey'.

On her arrival in Edmonton, she had to arrange Jack's funeral and put his things in order.

'It was a very sad occasion,' she says, 'being so soon after Jimmy had died.'

As Jack had died in somewhat suspicious circumstances, the police had to thoroughly investigate the cause of his death. In the end, it was put down to a heart attack.

On Friday 17 June 1977, Jack Earnest Hudson was cremated at the Park Memorial Chapel in Edmonton. The service was performed by the Reverend Tom Kroetch, who, by coincidence, was the local priest of May Diver, an old Group associate and good friend of both Jimmy and Jean.

Jean sorted out Jack's things and gathered together all she could that was of sentimental value, leaving the rest of his possessions to be auctioned off.

Among the mementoes kept by Jean today of her two friends are a clock and a chair. The clock, of French manufacture, had belonged to Jimmy. She remembers him telling her the story behind it.

'He went out on the stage of the Metropolitan Theatre in London,' recounts Jean, 'and he was very nervous. So, to calm himself, he looked down at the front two rows of the stalls, counted the customers and mentally bought the clock with the takings. He would do things like that. I'd known him to look dramatically towards the circle and announce that "there was the guts of a three-piece suite up there!"'

Jean also held on to a gold wrought iron and velvet chair, bought by Jimmy, but which Jack had asked her to keep when he left for Canada. The plan was that he would arrange for it to be sent over at a later date.

'I still have it in my living room,' she says, 'and, even though it's so heavy and could do with another coat of gold paint, it still brings back such lovely memories of Jimmy and how he was so worried before he started his one-man shows. He used to say, "How can I sit in the one place for two-and-a-half hours, after being used to moving all over the stage for so long?"'

Fernwood Street plaque

The Union Street plaque in Ballymoney, after corrections had been made

It's true to say that, while Jimmy's death devastated his devoted legion of fans at the time, he is far from forgotten today. As he said himself: 'The people of Belfast never forget. Sure, they still remember 1690!'

The fire that forged such memorable characters as Orange Lil, Mrs O'Condriac, Wee Ernie the shipyard worker, the Cherryvalley snob, and Billy Hulk the trade union leader, has clearly been kept alight.

Initially, this was achieved when the BBC and Emerald Music reissued audio and video recordings of Jimmy's stage and television shows. On their release, these cassettes, videos and CDs found a receptive audience, including many who were discovering Jimmy for the very first time.

On 26 October 1996, friends such as Mervyn Solomon and Ivan Martin, as well as Jimmy's former neighbours, gathered outside 26 Fernwood Street, where a plaque was unveiled by the Ulster History Circle to mark the house which had been his childhood home. Sadie Griffith, whose brothers used to play with Jimmy in the street, remarked at the time: 'He gave a lot of pleasure to a lot of people. He made you laugh at yourself. He was a man of the people, a great person.'

A year later, on 9 April 1997, the town of Ballymoney decided it was their turn to honour their celebrated son. Again, a plaque was unveiled, this time at 33 Union Street, the house where Jimmy had been born. Frank Crummey was in attendance at this unveiling which, as he points out, did not go exactly to plan.

'Ivan Martin and I were invited up to Ballymoney,' remembers Frank. 'There was a bit of a do at the town hall and then we went round to the house with a few of the councillors who were hosting the thing. So, they started to announce, "It is a great honour to unveil this plaque in honour of James Young, who was born in this house in 1918", and they unveiled the thing and – Holy Jesus – they'd the wrong flipping date on it! They had him dying in 1984 instead of 1974.

'So I said to Ivan, "Look at the date on it. Do you think we should tell them?" But the local punters didn't seem to notice. We discreetly informed the councillors, much to their embarrassment, and they got it fixed a few days later.'

On the 25th anniversary of Jimmy's death, Downtown Radio presented

The plaque placed in Jimmy's honour outside the Group Theatre

a tribute show, hosted by Ulster Television announcer, John O'Hara, who as an amateur actor all those years before, had first met Jimmy. On the show, O'Hara summed up what he believed Jimmy's legacy to be.

'His highly individual brand of humour focused, to a large extent, o the extremes in our attitudes and personalities, particularity in relation t religion and politics. One moment we were laughing at the absurdity of our perceived differences, the next he would bring a lump to the throat an tears to the eye with the pathos of a heartbreaking monologue, which spoke volumes about the realities of life and living together.'

Around this time, others lined up to pay tribute to Jimmy. Ivan Marti himself stated that Jimmy 'was the first person to characterise Belfas people. His humour crossed the divide and everyone saw their neighbou uncle, or brother in the characters he portrayed.'

Nuala McKeever, formerly of the Hole in the Wall Gang before strikin out on a successful solo career, added: 'He is one of the names alway mentioned when you talk about comedy and, as a performer, I wa inspired by him. His cheeky humour pushed the boundaries and h deserves to be revered and remembered.'

Reliving the old days. William Caulfield and Olivia Nash in A Tribute to James Young

Even the Reverend Ian Paisley, who ha been parodied by Jimmy in the past, had kind word to say: 'I am sure that Youn himself had no bitterness in his heart agains the people he took out on.'

That same year, a gold plaque wa unveiled at the entrance of the Grou Theatre, inscribed with the words: 'Th citizens of Belfast gratefully acknowledge th contribution made by Ulster comedian Jame Young to the life and humour of the city. H regarded the Group Theatre as his hom throughout the 1960s and 1970s.'

September 2001 saw Tyrone comedia and actor, William Caulfield, teaming u with one of Jimmy's old sidekicks, Olivi Nash, to appear in *Our Jimmy: A Tribute t*

James Young at the Group Theatre. The show was well received by critics and public alike and went on tour to rapturous approval around the country. While reinvigorating the sketches, songs and monologues which audiences had lapped up in the past, Caulfield always finished his Group shows with a monologue written by himself in the style of, and in tribute to, Jimmy.

> *I met a man on Bedford Street, aye, just the other day,*
> *Who stopped me for a minute or two to while some time away.*
> *We talked about the weather, as we in Ulster love to do*
> *And then he spoke of this place and, of course, of Jimmy too.*
> *For it seems no matter where I go, busy shop or in the street,*
> *All of you so loved him, and so you tell me when we meet.*
> *Each of you have your precious memories, of the laughter that he brought,*
> *And the tears he made you cry as well, when in monologue, he did talk.*
>
> *For embedded deep in Belfast, just as real as the City Hall,*
> *Is the memory of a genius beloved by one and all,*
> *Who, in this city's dark, dark history and all its troubled while,*
> *Never stopped believing in the unity of a smile.*
> *And in this very building, he paraded for all to see,*
> *A host of lovely characters, the spit of you and me.*
> *And through them, we learned the folly of the bigotry and hate.*
> *Yet, sad to say, for some that's a lesson not learned yet.*

Paying homage. William Caulfield straightens Jimmy's picture at the Group Theatre

But right in this here theatre, for indeed this was his home,
I'm standing where the master stood and you've not left me alone.
For tonight we've heard the laughter, and tonight we've shed a tear,
And somewhere out there he's listening for he's never far from here.
So thank you all for coming, for each have played your part,
And it's clear from where I'm standing: we still love James Young at heart

When asked to explain Jimmy's enduring popularity, William Caulfiel
points out: 'His material still works today because the sad thing is th
situation in Northern Ireland hasn't changed. We still haven't moved o
that much in 30 years, and that's why it has the same impact that it did a
those years ago.'

Amid all the tributes paid to Jimmy since his death – the televisio
documentaries, plays, newspaper and magazine articles, books, and so o
– one in particular stands out. Again, it is in the form of a plaque, bu
placed in a secret location, known only to a select few, somewhere i
Northern Ireland.

As he was unlikely to have children of his own, Jimmy's great dream wa
to be the godparent of one of his friend's children. He was overjoyec
therefore, when he was asked to assume that very role for Lorna Rebecc
McNeill, the daughter of his close friend, Leonard.

Leonard was a member of the Church of Ireland, which has a stric
requirement that godparents are also members. Jimmy had been raised a
a Presbyterian and, to become little Lorna's godfather, had to tak
instruction and be baptised in a formal ceremony. He was more than gla
to do this, but when the minister told Leonard that the person chosen t
be godmother was unsuitable, Leonard angrily decided not to have hi
child baptised at all and left it at that. Until very recently, he was totall
unaware of how badly Jimmy had taken this.

'Jimmy was quite upset about this and told me so,' says Jean. 'When m
daughter, Lorraine, heard that Jimmy had gone to all the trouble of takin
instruction for the Church of Ireland, which, incidentally, was our ow
church, she said to him, "Will you stop worrying? If I ever have a little gir
you can be her godfather. Provided, of course, that you go to churcl
regularly."

'This he did, and he became a very good member of the Church o
Ireland at Orangefield, which was close to Roddens Park, his home i
those days.'

Lorraine gave birth to a little girl in 1972 and named her Suzanne, o
Suzy for short. Much to Jimmy's delight, he became her godfather.

When Jimmy died, Jack Hudson went to *Camelot* and opened a specia
safe built into the wall. It had been specifically designed to hold importan

documents that he would need in the event of Jimmy's passing. To his amazement, there was only one document in the safe: the baptism papers for Suzy, with Jimmy's name as godfather.

Touched by this, Jack asked Jean and Lorraine if it would be possible, since he had taken on a lot of Jimmy's responsibilities following his death, to become Suzy's honorary godfather. Lorraine agreed.

Jean had, by this time, planted a cherry tree in Jimmy's honour in a place that had been very special to the both of them throughout their friendship. He had always been fond of cherry trees because of their beautiful blossoms. When Jack died, she planted another cherry tree alongside Jimmy's and assigned an ironmonger to design a plaque. This was eventually set between the two trees. The inscription on it reads simply: 'To Suzy's godfathers.'

This touching memorial, which stands in a secret location highlight the real affection that existed between Jimmy and Jean. When speaking c his death, she says:

'I lost a friend – a very, very good friend. But, on the other hand, I jus say to myself:

'He's gone to a room I cannot find,
But I know he was here because of the happiness he left behind.'

And, if truth be told, Jimmy's circle of friends, in death as in life, extend well beyond the immediacy of those who worked with him, or knew hir best. To the audiences and fans of his stage, radio and televisio appearances, he was also a friend. For, in many ways, James Young did nc die. He lives on still in the faces and laughter of the men and women c Northern Ireland who will forever have a special place in their hearts fo 'Our Jimmy'.